DIVINE RESILIENCE

DIVINE RESILIENCE

Discovering Our Strength in the
Ether of Love, Death, and Possibility

ERIK ALONZO FLADAGER

© 2023 by Erik Alonzo Fladager

All rights reserved. This book or any portion thereof may not be reproduced or used in any manner whatsoever without the express written permission of the publisher except for the use of brief quotations in a book review.

ISBN: 9798393491635

Contents

Foreword 7

An Inspiration 11
A Note from the Author 13
Am I Resilient Enough? 17
Memento Mori 33
Discovering Our Strength
in the Ether of Love, Death, and Possibility 53
The Crisis and Mystery of Identity 57
Endurance 77
What's Love Got to Do with It? 89
Let's Talk about Ether 97

In Conclusion 107
Afterword 113
Acknowledgments 121
Notes 123

Foreword

By Mike Gorman

REALIZED AS I sat down to write about Erik's new book that there's an irony here I was not aware of when he first asked me to write the foreword. Of course, as anyone would, I reacted to his question with an overwhelming sense of honor. Soon after, though, I was overcome with doubts. Was I even worthy of this chance to dive into his work before it was seen by the rest of the world? Was I worthy of his trust in my own resilience? A trust I was certainly not sure was earned. Who was I to speak of resilience itself, never mind someone else's deep reflection on it? I'll tell you.

For most of my life, I have struggled with my weight, and not in the "nagging twenty pounds that won't seem to go away" sense. I weighed over five hundred pounds, riding a rollercoaster of diet efforts and massive crashes leading to new peaks in a cycle that seemed endless. In 2010 I decided I needed to make a massive change as I was facing unemployment and barely able to walk into an office from my car, never mind have the stamina to last through an interview. So I did it. By my fortieth birthday in 2013, I was down over three hundred pounds. I had won the prize, apparently, and very quickly threw it away. In about six months, I put the weight back on. That's not a typo; I have the pictures to prove it. I had resigned myself to an early death and would just live the time I had left lost in my addiction to food. Four years later, I went to bed every night with a letter by my bedside intended for my family just in case I did not wake up. I was certain that death was circling but was not motivated to do anything about it—except write down platitudes I intended to soothe my family's pain but that really were about enabling my behavior. I like to say at this point God intervened, even though my faith was, let's just say, rusty at the time. A family situation awoke in me a drive to be there for the people I cared for, not out of obligation but from a place of self-awareness of who I wanted to be and who I was not at the time. I set off on yet another journey, aware of my past failures with an understanding that the missing piece had always been a sense of true purpose and mindfulness. Like most things in my life, I had usually approached weight loss as a passenger along for the ride and not the driver. This time was different from the get-go, and again I found success, losing over 250 pounds but also discovering, finally, a sense of purpose in my life. I started sharing my story and experiences, the dark moments and the victories, the struggles and the pain. I found ways to not only help myself but help others who resonated with my journey. It was through this experience I encountered Erik. I went on his podcast to discuss my life and found in him a spirit that was driven for connection and a person unafraid to examine the tough questions many of us work hard to avoid. He told me I inspired him, but the opposite is really the truth. Which brings me to the irony I mentioned above.

This book is certainly about resilience and the part that divinity can play in it, but on a deeper level, it is a specific call to action. Erik's words challenge us not only to define the place resilience has occupied in our lives but direct us to act on it. The irony is that this book is a journey my soul needed that I hadn't anticipated when I touched the first page. My doubts about my own resilience were filtered through the past regrets and lessons I had not yet learned. Erik has taught me here that resilience isn't just a quality or a strength we possess; it is about how we have lived every moment that we have here on earth.

There is power in the perspective I gained through the experience of reading this book. Less than twenty pages in, I had already filled two pages of a journal with questions I needed to ask myself. What did I need to learn from my life of gaining and losing hundreds of pounds? What role has my faith played in my resilience, and what role has denying that faith also played? I will spare you all of the details but hope you allow me the cliché here to say what I have taken from this opportunity given to me is inspiration. I have no doubts that you will feel the same when you finish it.

If you haven't read his first book, *Our Soul's Path*, you are about to discover that Erik Fladager is a man who walks in faith but does not require you to mimic his footsteps. Instead, he shares it with us in the hope of driving insight into his purpose of challenging our perspective and understanding of resilience. I am excited for you to now start this journey for yourself. Me? I have returned to a place of honor for this experience, with no doubt Erik knew what he was doing when he asked.

An Inspiration

I WANT TO thank the great American author Steven Pressfield for introducing me to many fascinating and inspiring ideas as a writer. It is because of him I was introduced to the following poem. It is the start of Homer's *Odyssey*, and it immensely impacted me on my creative journey while preparing this project. As I present to you this book, I pray that it finds you at the perfect time. As so many artists have come before me to inspire and teach, I wish to do the same. I found this poem to be a divine inspiration:

> O Divine Poesy, goddess, daughter of Zeus, sustain for me this song of the various-minded man who, after he had plundered the innermost citadel of hallowed Troy, was made to stay grievously about the coasts of men, the sport of their customs, good and bad, while his heart, through all the sea-faring, ached with an agony to redeem himself and bring his company safe home. Vain hope—for them. The fools! Their own witlessness cast them aside. To destroy for meat the oxen of the most exalted Sun, wherefore the Sun-god blotted out the day of their return. Make this tale live for us in all its many bearings, O Muse.
>
> —Homer's *Odyssey*, translation by T. E. Lawrence

A Note from the Author

First of all, I would like to say thank you if you have picked up this book and decided to give it a shot. I thought it would be a great idea to give you, the reader, a few things to think about and consider as you read. This book is my second in what seems to have become a series about the complexities of life. It all began with *Our Soul's Path*, which has led me to this work. So much was covered in that first book, but I knew there were so many ideas left on the table. There were so many connections, thoughts, and stories I thought of afterward. So here we are with this book. Just so you know, I am not your traditional writer. (*What is a traditional writer?* you might be thinking. I actually don't know, but I imagine it is someone who writes long and beautiful romance novels or deeply researched four-hundred-page *New York Times* bestsellers.) That is not me, and that is not this book. I did not go to school for journalism or English literature; I often look up how to spell words correctly, and I am always trying to figure out how to take an abstract idea and bring it to layman's terms because that is how I have best come to understand things. As you read this book, you will see that I am trying to make connections. That is my ultimate goal. I want to bridge the gap between a big idea and my heart. I hope that in the process of doing so, you will have something to take away as the reader. I am an extremely curious individual, and I love learning. My goal is to share my curiosity and what I have learned. I have been influenced by so many different authors, athletes, filmmakers, YouTubers, philosophers, and figures from the Bible and history, and I want nothing more in life than to share my own knowledge with as many people as possible.

You will notice that within every chapter, there could be several topics. I will often take a bigger topic and try to break it down into smaller ideas, and my hope is that it all ties together to make sense to you. This book aims to tackle the topic of resiliency and strength, hence the title: *Divine Resilience*. I use the word *divine* because I believe it is in the nature of divinity where we find our true strength and resiliency in this life.

I do have a faith and belief in God. After reading that sentence, you might be wondering a few things about me, such as, What does that mean? Are you a Christian? If so, what denomination? Who's God? Is it the same God I grew up with or some new age version? That word, *God*, has a lot of meaning. I couldn't possibly give a short, blanket response to those questions, because depending on the person, one will have a unique thought about it. Because the truth is, I cannot define faith or God for you. All I can do is share my experiences, thoughts, feelings, and revelations and see where it takes us. I mention all of this because there is no way I could write about any topic such as this and not mention how God has been involved in my life. Just so you know, my faith in God does not mean I am here to preach to you either. I do not see it as my place to convince you of anything. I am going to do what my fifth-grade teacher, Mrs. Linsacum, told me never to do and that is assume. Enough people and institutions have tried to convince you already. Rather, I am here to share an experience. As you read each section and work your way through the book, my hope would be that the book creates a feeling within you. This feeling is hard to describe, but I will do my best.

You know that feeling you get when you read something or listen to someone, and you have this moment of clarity? You get this sort of *ahh, yes* moment? What you just read or heard made complete and total sense in your heart, and if you had to explain it to somebody else, it would be so hard because it isn't quantifiable. It isn't something so easily explained because it is…well…a feeling. That is what I am chasing in life. A feeling. I have a direction and a state of flow, and I am all in. *Our Soul's Path* was part of that direction and state of flow. (If you haven't read it, I highly recommend it. Wink, wink.) That is what I want for you. If you read this book and have one moment where this feeling is generated within you, then it was all worth it for me. I hold this so near and dear to my heart because I was on the receiving end of those moments all of my life. I have read countless books where I was struck with this feeling of inspiration, love, clarity, and energy. These moments are built into my foundation, and it is important to note that as a result I have much more resiliency and inner strength now than I ever did before. So not only do I want you to experience this feeling, but it is my personal belief that it is the key to anybody desiring to secure more resiliency, more strength, and a better understanding of themselves. So please, enjoy the book. Share what you find worthy and useful. Use it to add to the collective healing consciousness that we are all plugged into.

▲

Last note: all scripture used in the book is the New International Version unless stated otherwise, and the poems you will find between chapters are of free public domain.

Time is the king of all men, he is their parent and their grave, and gives them what he will and not what they crave.

—Pericles, Athenian general and politician, d. 429 BC

Am I Resilient Enough?

I'VE FOUND MYSELF asking this question many times throughout my life. I am sure if you picked up this book, you may have thought the same thing. You might have read the title on the cover and instantly thought of a time in your life that pushed you to your limit and called everything you thought you knew about yourself into question. That situation could have been from something major, like the death of a loved one, losing your job, the ending of a marriage, the folding of business, or an unexpected health crisis. Maybe it is not as serious. Maybe for you, this question comes to mind as you continuously grind each day against life's clock. So many of us are hyperbusy. There is always something going on, and you are always making yourself available and taking on more than you may be able to handle. You feel burnt out, lost, disoriented, and perhaps a bit worn down by all the craziness the world throws at us. Maybe you are in a season of questions right now. Life throws a variety of painstaking situations at us that often leave us asking:

Do I have the strength to get through this?
Do I have what it takes?
Why was I chosen for this?

The questions and thoughts never stop coming. The situations will never cease, yet they are what push us forward along the journey. If you are anything like me, you will be presented with life's wild and mysterious confrontations, roadblocks, barriers, twists, and turns and will wonder whether you have what it takes to keep going. In thirty years of living life, I thought I knew what I was truly made of, but the truth is that I am still trying to figure it out. What I have also learned is that it is completely OK not to have all the answers. We all have an innate ability for self-discovery. At some point we will hopefully all realize that we are, in fact, resilient enough to deal with the heaviest and the most painful points of contention in life and that they are the biggest building blocks we will ever receive. I have learned in my own life that the ability for healing, growth, and discovery is found in a loving and benevolent divinity that resides closely within each and every one of us. This is mostly what *Our Soul's Path* is about. What I also believe is that there is a sacred space between us all. There is a space between you and the problem and between you and the solution. There is sacred space in between *everything*. This is where we have the opportunity to discover our strength and grow from it. I refer to this space in this book as the ether of love, death, and possibility.

A PERSONAL EXAMPLE

At the time of this writing, my daytime job is as the school leader (or principal) of an alternative, credit-recovery high school in Phoenix, Arizona. As the school leader, I am confronted with challenges and problems all day long. It sort of comes with the territory. I put out fires each school day; I am tasked with strategizing and casting a vision for the school, and it is my job to make sure we move in that direction. When you work in public education, you see, hear, and experience a lot of things. You see trauma walk through your doors every single day. You are constantly bombarded with solving highly emotional and sensitive issues, and the truth is there is no type of education or training that prepares you for this. Like anything, you sort of learn the most through experience and working with experienced individuals. One moment you are in a meeting about data, rules, regulations, testing dates, this year's expectations, and so forth, and the next moment you are finding out that one of your students is living in an abusive situation. How do you absorb that information and simply move forward?

I remember clearly one afternoon driving home, I noticed that the road was shut down, and there was major traffic. I had to detour, and the roads were a mess. I remember thinking, *I wonder what happened?* Well, the following week I found out that one of our former students was killed in a motor vehicle accident. That was why the road was shut down on my way home. A kid I knew. A kid I really enjoyed having on campus. *A teenager.* He'd just turned eighteen.

So when I think about resilience, one parent in particular comes to my mind. I will not give names for obvious reasons, but during one of the school's breaks, there was a tragic incident involving a student of ours. A sixteen-year-old student was shot and killed. When this student did not show up for school and we heard the rumors, it was devastating. My staff and I spoke with this student's mother, and as she struggled to muster up the words on the phone, everyone's heart broke for her. News that is tragic usually doesn't even feel real in the moment.

Losing anybody is hard. Losing a child seems unimaginable. He literally had had his sixteenth birthday that same week. I bring this up because when I talk about the heaviness of life and resilience, this is a real-world example of the heavy. This is an example of wondering if you are strong enough, resilient enough, to go on and still find meaning and value and joy and love. At this student's viewing and celebration of life, I remember listening to his mother speak. She spoke with so much love, passion, and reverence. She spoke about the joy her son had brought her and how much she looked forward to seeing him again in the afterlife one day. She had so much strength. It was one of the bravest things I have ever witnessed in person. She was a walking, talking example of strength and resilience.

RESISTANCE

There is so much possibility between us and the problem that causes us discomfort. There is so much mastery to be learned when we deeply reflect on the areas of our heart and life where we find doors of resistance. Because resistance shows us where we are not OK with something. Resistance shows us where we are not OK with ourselves or with someone else. But it is the doorway of resistance where we must enter. Where there is resistance, there is much to learn and grow. There is so much to learn from the equation of life. We must be open to receiving it and engaging with it. I have learned this through much trial and error. What I have learned is that I need to engage with this resistance and seek the activity and challenge in all of it. The first moment I did, everything changed.

STRENGTH

I have spent a lot of time reading, studying, praying, and journaling about strength. Because at the core of the question "Am I resilient enough?" are additional questions about strength. I know I am not the only person to ever wonder if they have the strength to keep moving forward. Do I have the mental, emotional, and physical strength? We all have our moments where we feel like we have hit a limit. I mean, we literally have sayings such as, "I was at my breaking point," "I have had it up to here," and "I've lost my mind." Well, you get the picture. At these points of contention, we may be left to ponder these questions: What is my source of strength? Is it genetic? Is it tied to my faith? Is it something I can learn? If you haven't asked these questions, then maybe you should.

When seeking some wisdom, I often refer to ancient scriptures, poems, letters, and books that are found in the beautiful collection of stories otherwise known as the Bible. Within this collection, we find many themes around strength. Oftentimes, we fear we are losing our grasp on our life, but maybe it is because we are clinging to it with white-knuckle desperation. The harder we squeeze and the more energy we expend, the more we lose control of it. We say statements like, "I have tried everything," "I am doing everything that I can," and "I tried that."

It's like squeezing a bar of soap.

Where is our strength? It is certainly not found in desperation and our failed attempts to hold onto our problems with everything we have. I think we can all recall examples of times we tried and failed at this. Is our job crazy and overwhelming? Some of us work twelve hours a day instead of the usual eight in order to get caught up or ahead of things. We work the weekends away. We work while on vacation. We try to get ahead of it, though can you ever actually get ahead with work? How many have crashed and burned because of this mentality? How many people have broken themselves with this pursuit? Where is our strength?

If we go check in with this incredible and often misunderstood book called the Bible, we find one example from a very well-known story of a man by the name of Jesus. When Jesus is taken to the cross and is crucified, his final words are: "'Father, into your hands I commit my spirit.' When he had said this, he breathed his last" (Luke 23:46).

It is generally thought Jesus was actually quoting scripture himself—Psalm 31:5, to be exact:

> In you, Lord, I have taken refuge;
> let me never be put to shame;
> deliver me in your righteousness.
> Turn your ear to me,
> come quickly to my rescue;
> be my rock of refuge,
> a strong fortress to save me.
> Since you are my rock and my fortress,
> for the sake of your name lead and guide me.
> Keep me free from the trap that is set for me,
> for you are my refuge.
> Into your hands I commit my spirit;
> deliver me, Lord, my faithful God.

Where is our strength?
I believe it to be found in the act of releasing.
Relinquishing.
Handing the problem over.

There is this false notion that we can control all of the outcomes in life. Our strength can be found in releasing our control to this idea, because in fact, we cannot control all of the outcomes. Yes, we can and do control what we say, how we act, and how we behave. But this does not mean that we control any sort of outcome in life. There are too many other deciding factors at play. There are other people and their decisions to consider as well.

So when I ask this constant question, "Where is our strength?", I can honestly say that I believe there is strength in relinquishing our problems, worries, anxieties, and life to God's love and the infinite possibilities that lie ahead. Instead of burning ourselves out with a death grip on our perceived issues, we should hand over control to something greater. "Into your hands I commit my spirit," says Jesus as he dies on the cross.

How does "Into your hands I commit my spirit" look in your life?

In what areas can you say, "I release" and truly mean it?

It is not easy, and it will be an uphill battle for many. But if you are someone who read the title of this book and it nudged you in the slightest way possible, then I believe you should do a deep dive of the self and see where you can release control. Continuing to burn the candle on both ends only to flame out before your truest potential is revealed would be a devastation to the world.

WE'RE ALL A WORK IN PROGRESS

This is the second book I have written. Before this book, I sunk an enormous amount of time and energy into *Our Soul's Path*. What it took from me to write that book and bring it to life was vast. Naturally, when I got the idea to write the second book, I felt scared. I got a tinge of anxiety and worry.

I am not even finished with my first book, I thought.

I don't even know how the first book will sell. Why am I already writing a second?

Our Soul's Path *took hundreds of hours to put together. Are you ready to do that again?*

All of these thoughts flooded my mind. All of these thoughts are valid and completely normal but are terrifying at the same time. This second book was like a thorn in my side. I kept feeling it, thinking of it, and daydreaming about it, like I was being told over and over that it needed to be written. I just wanted to take a rest and feel accomplished after completing my first book, but sitting on the sidelines wasn't in the cards. So there I was at my desk, answering the call for yet another book.

ANOTHER CHALLENGE

I still remember the day the idea was planted in my head to write this book. It first came to me as a word. I was in the middle of a run one day after work. Usually I run in the evening when I get off from work, and it is my time to listen to some of my favorite music and go Zen. I pray, I think, I wonder, I daydream, I feel the physical pain of the run mixed with the emotional runner's high you get from letting your body free flow for close to an hour. I was praying about my first book. Specifically, I prayed for patience and wisdom. I prayed for God's love and healing energy to flow through my hands and head and onto the page. I kept thinking repeatedly how special this moment in time was. Not only did I write *Our Soul's Path*, but I got experience. This process of prayer, meditation, work, running, and then the chance to write it all down was a great challenge. *What an opportunity this is*, I thought.

Then it hit me. At first, it was just a word. A powerful word: *resilience*. As I dwelled on that word, it then shifted to *divine resilience*. Even though I wasn't completely done writing the first book, I knew I had another idea to act upon. A new book to write. It was all a surreal rush. I still had more to complete, more with which to work forward.

Moving forward.

Sometimes, failing forward.

Moving, nonetheless.

This new idea had me thinking and reflecting on so many things I was experiencing currently. It was time for more self-examination. This word, *resiliency*. What did it really mean to me? What does it mean to others?

AM I RESILIENT ENOUGH?

Oftentimes, I find myself in a holding pattern. I wind up in circumstances where I feel as if I am waiting and waiting. If you are accustomed to movement and productivity, it is hard to wait. I feel as if there is no progress if I am simply waiting. I get the sense that I may even be regressing if I am waiting. Simply put, waiting drives me crazy. There have been numerous times in my life, professionally speaking, where this has been apparent. I am almost certain many of you reading this book have felt the same way at one point or another. Throughout my career, I have been blessed to be put in a position of leadership wherever I've been. I have been given opportunities time and time again to lead and to serve, and for that I am eternally grateful. However, whenever I have been tasked with doing the same job for months or even years at a time, like many of you, I become bored. I am the type of person who wants to grow, who wants to be challenged. I enjoy variety. I like to be engaged. Maybe my ego doesn't want to be hurt, but I know challenge is the only way to truly advance in this life. So when I was first given the position of dean of students at the school I was working at, it was a huge responsibility to me. I felt the weight of that responsibility and wanted to take that position and run with it. As difficult as it was, I embraced the challenge and tried to learn from every difficult moment on the job. It had thrilling moments and moments that terrified me. Sometimes I had no clue what I was doing, but I was learning through every situation. Growing through every high-stress situation. I had moments that tested every ounce of patience I had and moments where I felt like I was exactly where God intended me to be.

So. Many. Moments.

After several school years in that job, I felt ready for a new challenge. I had spent six years in one place, the longest I had stayed anywhere before.

Six years serving students.

Six years serving teachers.

Six years building momentum.

Six years developing people.

Six years handling crisis situations.

Six years of giving suspensions.

Six years of unclogging toilets, mopping floors, pulling weeds, substitute teaching, mending broken desks, building new ones, repurposing classrooms, training new people, and filling any gap necessary.

I knew it was a good job by many standards. I was well respected and had a great routine, but I was too complacent. I couldn't quite shake the feeling of being either bored or frustrated with the work. Don't get me wrong; there was always more work to do at the school, people to hire, broken stuff needing mending, students needing help, and faculty needing support. I just thought I had had my fill. I felt like it was work for someone new, someone fresh, to do. I prayed and meditated on it daily. I truly felt ready to be plucked out from that position and placed somewhere else.

I was *tired*.

Deflated.

Willing for something new.

I did what anyone would do in that situation: I began a long and difficult journey to try and find a new path. I searched for new careers and jobs; I put in applications; I sent in my resume; and I researched a plethora of new situations, companies, and industries to immerse myself in.

I received rejection email after rejection email.

I was told I was not an ideal candidate.

I didn't have enough experience.

I was told they were looking for someone with more education.

"We are looking for a candidate with education in a field we feel is more related."

I had numerous prescreen phone calls with HR professionals. Some led to an interview, and some sat in limbo for weeks until I got the inevitable email stating they had decided to move forward with "other highly qualified candidates."

Then there were the interviews I had…oh, the interviews. The interviews would seem to go well, but they, too, led to further rejection. This was so confusing and conflicting for me. I thought I was being led to move on. I thought the divine was preparing my heart for something else, so why was I hitting so many walls? Making the decision to end my time as dean was so difficult to make. I had this major conflict in my heart and soul. I knew it was a safe and comfortable job.

A job that provided so much for me.

A job that I knew like the back of my hand.

A job where I was a resource for so many people.

But here I was, waiting.

Stuck in a holding pattern.

There's that word again: *stuck. If I am stuck, am I regressing?* I thought. *Why would God put it in my heart to leave, then keep me at the very same place?* This was my dilemma. After every rejection, after every attempt at something new, I had to accept waiting all over again. What I started to learn was that I was not in control. I could not predict the future, and I needed to stand firm in my resiliency and be open to learning from it all. Rather than feel frustration, I should feel excitement. The only thing I could ask of myself was to listen and try. I had to accept that I did not know the timeline or sequence of events. My part was to listen and try again. I was learning that resiliency was the act of effort, diligence, and intention combined with time. While we can control our efforts, diligence, and intentions, time, on the other hand, is a mystery. The length of time we think is necessary to learn or grow may not be what is actually needed to prepare us for the road ahead.

So I had a choice to make. I could give up on the effort and stay put in my career, hoping for something to materialize. I could continually hope each opportunity I sought would work out and feel dejected when it didn't. Or I could accept that the timeline is completely out of my control and focus my heart on listening and acting. I needed to keep pressing, trying, going, and moving, and not keep count of the scoreboard. I couldn't have planned it, but when I let it be, the opportunity to become the principal opened up. Part of me felt like I was not ready. Part of me was scared. But the opportunity presented itself, nonetheless. Becoming the principal led me right back to a simple question…

AM I RESILIENT?

I've heard many say that life is a marathon, not a sprint. That is true. But in the moment-to-moment reality that we live in, I am sure many feel as if they are sprinting and sprinting and sprinting without any true destination in sight.

How tiresome.

We cannot sprint our way through a marathon. That's also not the point. If we are to wade through the waters of life, then finding the inner strength to keep going is our prerogative. I've met many who have endured the draining experiences of divorce, sickness, abuse, rejection, and addiction. Some say, "To live and to be human is to suffer." Many of you will read that line and will nod in agreement. It reminds me of that saying that we are either approaching a storm, in the middle of one, or just exiting one. That is life on earth. That is also what makes us so resilient. Some may feel hopeless. Don't. You have the capacity to deal with anything life throws at you. Deep within our heart is the strength to deal with it all. You just need to unlock it. And it's not as hard as we may think.

What I have learned through this whole process is that I have a reservoir of resilience and self-discovery rooted in my identity—endurance, death, and life. I will elaborate on each, and we will enter a journey into the world of acceptance, love, divinity, and self-mastery. It is my greatest hope that God's resiliency radiates through the words and chapters of this book and onto you so that you can take away something valuable and fight the good fight in your life's journey.

This is why this book is titled *Divine Resiliency*. Because, ultimately, I have come to find the source of our strength and resiliency rooted in the divine. I have learned about strength and resiliency through a multitude of experiences and education. This is why, throughout the book, you will find a mixture of subjects on the topics of identity, endurance, memento mori, wisdom from the Bible, personal experiences I have had, and the significance of the word *ether* in the subtitle.

I always try to make one thing clear to people when we speak or when they read my work: I am no guru. I am nobody special. I do not hold ultimate authority in the subject of resilience. Rather, I am rigorous in my pursuit to understand life, and I am deeply passionate about people. I am a lifelong learner and want nothing more than to teach, serve, and learn from others. I hold my passions close to my heart and want nothing more in life than to know that I helped some people understand their situations a little bit better.

INVICTUS

By William Ernest Henley

Out of the night that covers me,
Black as the pit from pole to pole,
I thank whatever gods may be
For my unconquerable soul.

In the fell clutch of circumstance
I have not winced nor cried aloud.
Under the bludgeonings of chance
My head is bloody, but unbowed.

Beyond this place of wrath and tears
Looms but the Horror of the shade,
And yet the menace of the years
Finds and shall find me unafraid.

It matters not how strait the gate,
How charged with punishments the scroll,
I am the master of my fate,
I am the captain of my soul.

Memento Mori

IT IS SAID that when a Roman general would come home from a major victory, there would be a daylong or multiple-day celebration, and it would often result in a sacrifice at a sacred temple. Some of these rituals and sacrifices took place at the illustrious Temple of Jupiter Optimus Maximus or at the glorious Temple of Saturn, both on Capitoline Hill in Rome. Upon that staggering hill, the Romans placed numerous altars, statues, and trophies on display. The victorious general would parade through the streets of the city, donning the finest of clothes and gold. During the parade, through the awe-inspiring streets of Ancient Rome, this general—who eventually became Caesar—would have a commoner or slave follow him and whisper the phrase *memento mori* into his ear. Memento mori can be translated as "Remember that you die," or "Remember that you must die." This is a reminder that it does not matter if you are a king, Caesar, a decorated general, a philosopher, or a common man or woman. The same fate faces us all. When we think of death, most of us try to block it out, because it is such an overwhelming thought to concentrate on. Or we think death is a distant inevitability better kept in a faraway locker somewhere, never to be thought of or examined. The truth is that we do in fact all die in the flesh here on earth, and that is OK. In fact, if we look at it the right way, it is more than OK. Looking at death differently can be the source of tremendous strength, courage, and resilience.

QUID MEIPSUM—~~WHY ME?~~

So many of us will find ourselves in a season of life that may be extremely hard and lonely. We might be in a situation we never asked for, and it leaves us asking the proverbial question, Why me?

How did this happen?

What is the purpose or meaning?

Where do I find the strength to be resilient in all of this?

Hard questions to ask. Even harder answers to understand. Maybe for you, it's not that black and white. It's not a season or an event. Life is pretty good, but there is a lingering question in your mind, a feeling in your gut. It's like that quote from Henry David Thoreau: "Most men lead lives of quiet desperation." Perhaps that is something we all face, the quiet desperation. Living without a true barometer is to be alive. This is why I believe that knowing the simple truth of memento mori pushes us into the process of answering those questions and realizing the gift of life. I believe those questions and our human instinct to seek out resilience are as old as time. Our humanity is ancient, so why not go to the source for clarity?

I have read a lot in my short life and yet I have barely scratched the surface when it comes to the sheer volume of useful information and influential people out there. So many people throughout time and history dealt with the exact same thoughts, worries, and situations and expressed themselves though writing in order to cement their knowledge for eternity. So many beautiful and poetic sources and walks of life to choose from. King David, Marcus Aurelius, Homer,

Seneca, Paul the Apostle, Hemingway, Melville, Tolstoy, C. S. Lewis, and Virginia Woolf, to name a few. When I meditated on this subject of memento mori and dug a little deeper, I found a few other sources that touched on the same concept. According to the Catholic canonized version of the Old Testament, there is a book called the Book of Ecclesiasticus (not found in Judaism or Protestant versions of the Old Testament, mind you). According to *Britannica*, it was thought to have been authored under the pen names of "Ben Sira" or "Jesus Sirach" around 180–175 BC.[2] The verse reads, "In all thy works remember thy last end, and thou shalt never sin" (Ecclesiasticus [Sirach] 7:40 DRC, 1752).

I heard something really cool recently that has a lot to do with that verse and the idea of memento mori. An elderly man walks up to a young married couple and asks them how they are doing. The young couple says that they are good. The elderly gentleman begins to pry a bit and asks them if they are happy with their lives. The couple says yes, but then they begin to explain that they deal with the usual stuff and the typical difficulties of life. They work hard, wish they would make more money, wish they had fewer problems, wish they had more time together, wish they had more time to do the things they really enjoy. He likes to hike; she likes to paint. But who has time for that truly? After explaining this to the elderly man, he asks them how they would feel if he were to gift them $1 million. They both agreed they would be ecstatic, happy, and relieved, and it would be a thing to celebrate. The elderly man asks, "What about $10 million?" The couple smile and laugh and agree that would be even better. It would change their lives forever. Then the man says, "What if it meant you couldn't wake up tomorrow morning?" The smiles drain from the couple's face, and they say it wouldn't be worth it at all. In fact, no amount of money or treasure would be worth that. The man follows up with, "Are you both guaranteed to wake up tomorrow morning?" The couple look at each other and say, "No, I guess not." The elderly man says, "Exactly. You have no idea when your last day is, and you both agree that you would rather wake up tomorrow morning than have $10 million. So then why don't you wake up every morning with a huge sense of joy? Energy? Vigor?"

"In all thy works, remember thy last end" radiates through my head as I recall that story. How often am I caught wallowing in my own self-pity? In my own first world nonsense? I am ashamed to say, far too often. However, I have this verse. I have this story. I have this new insight to keep me focused on what actually matters. It is like I cannot stress it enough to myself, and maybe you are the same way. Everything that you believe is a stressor or a worry would most likely vanish if I were to tell you that you were not waking up tomorrow. Even though there is a good chance that you will, there is also a legitimate chance that you won't.

THE WISEST MAN

As I read more verses, they sent me down a path to the book of Ecclesiastes, written by King Solomon, also known as the wisest man to have ever lived. There is a section that reads:

> It is better to go to a house of mourning than to go to a house of feasting, for death is the destiny of everyone; the living should take this to heart. Frustration is better than laughter, because a sad face is good for the heart. The heart of the

wise is in the house of mourning, but the heart of fools is in the house of pleasure.

—Ecclesiastes 7:2–4

Backward thinking maybe? Did you struggle with that one as I did when first reading it? King Solomon was known for his immense wisdom, hence his nickname. But this isn't by random chance or a name he was given by a few buddies for always knowing to bet against the Dallas Cowboys in a playoff game (sorry to my fellow Cowboys fans). No, there are volumes of wisdom in this statement here, starting with "for death is the destiny of everyone" and its relation to the house of mourning. The house of mourning is another way to say *funeral*. Get familiar with it. We've all been to one, I would imagine. We will all have one, in some form or another. The fool is obsessed with only the pleasures in life. When we are hyperfocused on the pleasures—the feasting, the wining and dining—anything that comes in between us and the pleasure will cause us despair. He says, "Frustration is better than laughter, because a sad face is good for the heart." Here's an example:

I go to the airport; it's busy. The security line is long, my bag gets flagged, and I have to dump everything out. The flight is delayed forty-five minutes, and there is a crying baby next to me on the flight. Sounds like a typical airport experience. Frustrating, but typical. First, should I have expected everything to go perfectly when going to the airport? Do the words airport and perfect even go together? The experience is frustrating all the same, but how I respond is where the fool and the wise part ways. The fool will allow it to ruin their day. They will tell everyone possible about the terrible experience. They will become short tempered with their significant other. They will allow it to dampen their experience once landing. They will tweet, post, text, share, and reshare the experience to anybody willing to join in on the toxicity. They must have expected everything to go smoothly. Perfectly. They may have already been thinking about the expensive dinner they were going to have after landing and what new thing they were going to buy and how it was going to momentarily fulfill them until the next shiny thing came along. "Frustration is better than laughter, because a sad face is good for the heart." But the wise person takes it in stride. The wise person is frustrated like anybody would be, but the wise knew going to the airport would involve a long line. A potential for a flight delay. A crying baby. Dysfunctional security checkpoints. The wise person has been here before and understands it all comes with the territory, and more importantly, that it doesn't matter. The wise person is alive. Breathing. Has a good book or a music playlist. The wise person laughs because it will make for a fun story to tell, and they anticipate the laughter and joy it will bring their loved ones when they exaggerate how long the line was, how loud the baby was, and how awful the plane smelled. Because it is good for the soul to be hyperaware of the fleeting nature of life and our place in it. You are here, alive, reading this. What a gift it is. King Solomon was one wise man.

The same fate befalls us all. "Remember thy last end." When we think about our resilience and our trials, we must do it with the end in mind. When we are in the throes of victory or defeat, I know it can be difficult to shift our focus and our outlook and think about death. It feels inauspicious. But we can learn from the greats, the ones who came before us and grappled with the same issues. In his book *Meditations*, Marcus Aurelius wrote to himself, "You could leave life right now. Let that determine what you do and say and think."[1] If we are to build lasting resilience in ourselves, then we must have a greater perspective of life and of the road ahead. We are told that the heart of the wise is in the house of mourning. This house of mourning and the recognition that death is our destiny provides us immense perspective; with that perspective comes an unmatched level of energy. This is the energy we will summon to push through all the challenges life has to offer. Therefore, I will call on anyone reading this book right now to reflect...

Are you behaving with the end in mind?

What is your perspective each day?

What does memento mori mean to you?

Marcus Aurelius in *Meditations* writes again:

> Concentrate every minute like a Roman—like a man—on doing what's in front of you with precise and genuine seriousness, tenderly, willingly, with justice. And on freeing yourself from all other distractions. Yes, you can—if you do everything as if it were the last thing you were doing in your life, and stop being aimless, stop letting your emotions override what your mind tells you, stop being hypocritical, self-centered, irritable. You see how few things you have to do to live a satisfying and reverent life? If you can manage this, that's all even the gods can ask of you.[1]

PREPARE FOR GLORY

In the 2007 Zach Snyder action film *300*, there is this incredible scene toward the end of the movie between

King Leonidas (portrayed by Gerard Butler) and his fellow Spartans. In the movie, three hundred Spartans defend the *hot gates* of Thermopylae against a Persian invasion led by King Xerxes; however, actual history suggests that thousands of Greeks went to fight, and it was three hundred Spartans with Leonidas who bravely stayed behind to form a rear guard against the surrounding Persian forces so that a retreat could be made by the other Greeks. To give some more context as to why the Persians were invading Greece at this time (546 BC), it is important to know that the Persian empire was the world superpower. They had been the dominant force in the world for some time, and they had a bone to pick with Greece because of some drama Xerxes's father, King Darius, had with the Greeks. King Darius already tried to invade Greece once and was unsuccessful, as he was defeated at the Battle of Marathon by an Athenian general by the name of Themistocles (coolest name ever, right?). It must have been pretty embarrassing for the Persian empire, so naturally, there was some major turmoil between the Persians and Greek city-states, thus prompting King Xerxes to set out on another invasion to crush Greece.

The movie is a personal favorite because it is filled with all sorts of wild and bloody fight scenes, great one-liners, and its fair share of historically inaccurate moments. But out of all the scenes that drew my attention, one in particular stands out. As legend tells it, the Spartans were completely outnumbered. They were fighting with one distinct tactical advantage—bunkering in this narrow pass known as the *hot gates*. It was in this narrow pass that the Persian numbers did not matter as much, and it suited the Spartan fighting style of utilizing a powerful phalanx. However, there was another route the Persians could take to outflank the Spartans. Unfortunately, due to a traitor among their ranks, the Persians found out and the Spartans lost their great tactical advantage. They were still outnumbered, and now they were surrounded, with no way out. Then comes this perfect line in the movie. The line that I'm sure everyone who has seen the movie can hear in their head as they read it. Just after being told about their imminent defeat by an ally, facing all of his men, King Leonidas says the following: "Spartans! Prepare for glory!"[4]

Why bring this up? Because King Leonidas was not referring to glory as in winning the battle. He knew they were all going to die. Their glory would be found in death, and they were going to live and fight and not shy away from the guarantee of death. Like I mentioned earlier, I know this is a movie, and there is no way to know if the real King Leonidas shouted anything remotely close to this during the actual clash roughly twenty-five hundred years ago. But I love that scene so much because of this grand idea. This idea that we can view our end as glorious. It is not that the actual act of dying itself is glorious. I do not want to confuse the two. Dying in battle may make for a good movie scene or book, but true war is hell on earth. So what I am referring to is this notion that the inevitability of death and living purposefully with that in mind is glorious, and what happens afterward, in my humble opinion, is a touch above glory as well.

I mean, can you imagine? Let's just think for a moment. You are a Greek warrior and have been fighting with very little sleep, food, or water, and you have been driven to exhaustion—the type of exhaustion that we can't even conceive of in our modern-day worldview. You find out that you are surrounded, with absolutely no way to win. If everyone tries to desert the battlefield and run, the enemy forces will catch up and annihilate the lot of you. So you volunteer to form a rear guard with your king so that as many Greeks as possible can escape. You see the glory in it. You have the luxury of knowing the exact moment in which your time runs out, and with that information, you act. You act boldly and bravely. You take necessary action. You fight back. You make the most with what little time you have left. It's glorious. It reminds me of this scripture that King David wrote:

> Yet I am always with you; you hold me by my right hand. You guide me with your counsel, and afterward you will take me into glory.
>
> —Psalm 73:23–24

There we have it again, so beautifully written: "And afterward you will take me into glory." Whether it be in history, movies, or ancient scripture, I have been moved by these notions of viewing the ending as glorious. But what does this have to do with resilience? Strength? I would answer those questions with another question. I'm sure you have heard this saying before: "What's the worst that could happen?"

Most would say that the worst thing that could happen in life is…you die. That's probably the worst thing that could happen.

Death is scary. The thought of leaving this planet behind and leaving all of our loved ones behind is not something many of us want to focus on. Losing somebody is equally difficult to think about and conceptualize as well. So many of us have experienced these hardships of losing a close loved one all too early. Or maybe it wasn't too early. Some of us have grandparents and great-grandparents whom we love dearly and have had many years with, and their departure is just as sad because they were such a rock in our lives.

Just as I said that the moment of death itself is not glorious, neither is the feeling of loss. There is a heartache associated with loss which may not be comparable to anything else on the planet. More heartache and sorrow are not what I'm advocating for. There is plenty of that to go around. Although I think all pain has the opportunity to fortify our soul and give us a grander perspective on life, the seed I want to sow into everyone is the combination of death and glory. Both of them together, sealed and cemented into our minds and hearts.

Death is inescapable. If nature has her way, we do not get to choose the day, the hour, or the particular moment. What would happen in your life if you lived with the end in mind? How would you and could you be different if you operated under the principle that you are headed *for glory* and *into glory*?

What's the worst that could happen?

I can speak from my own point of view. The moment I realized that the end was not something to fear or worry about but rather a reason to live with nothing held back, everything changed. It's what the kids would call a game changer. For me, I was known to hold back and not say what was truly on my mind or do what I actually wanted to do. But I am headed into glory. I am headed for glory. So why would I hold back?

SO WHY MEMENTO MORI?

I would first ask anyone to write down those words—memento mori. Write it on a piece of paper or in your journal, or type it into a note on your phone. I would also challenge you, whether you are religious or not, to reread that scripture in Ecclesiastes and search for its meaning for yourself. See what stands out to you and how it can be applied in your heart. Whether you are secular or nonsecular, spiritual but not religious, or spiritual and religious, it doesn't matter. These ancient texts were written by real people with real worries and real lives. Thus, I have found such a deep connection to it and its meaning. I believe narratives and wisdom pop up throughout humanity for a purpose and a reason. I believe they can be used as a guide for us. If we are brave enough to connect the dots, we can begin to build and scaffold its architecture and bring it to life through the way we choose to act.

MORE FROM THE STOICS

Marcus Aurelius was not the only Roman Stoic to ponder these ideas about life and death either. We also have Seneca, who wrote in his moral letters to Lucilius, "Let us prepare our minds as if we'd come to the very end of life. Let us postpone nothing. Let us balance life's books each day…The one who puts the finishing touches on their life each day is never short of time." For those who do not know a whole lot about Seneca, I will do my best to give him some justice and provide a brief background. I'm not as good as podcaster Dan Carlin, but I will give it a shot. From my understanding, Seneca was born approximately the same time as Jesus Christ and was even believed to be in Rome at the same time as Paul, formerly known as Saul (writer of Galatians, Romans, and Corinthians, to name a few). He had been both a banished and an exiled man under Emperor Claudius, whereas he was a wealthy man under Emperor Nero. It appears he had seen and lived on both ends of the spectrum in his life. His unfortunate exile came at the hands of Claudius. As story tells it, Seneca was accused of adultery with Claudius's niece, Julia Livilla, and spent about eight years in exile as a result. It was in exile that he produced many wonderful letters and essays, one of which was to his mother to console her. When he was finally able to return to Rome, it is said he did so at the request of Claudius's wife so that he could tutor her son and future emperor, Nero Claudius Caesar Augustus Germanicus (that's a mouthful). It was under Nero's rule that Seneca held a variety of positions and obtained his wealth. But in the end, Seneca is said to have been forced by Nero to take his own life. An ordered suicide from the emperor himself. He had been accused of taking part in a plot to kill Nero. As the story tells it, when Seneca was given this order, he did not appeal it. It is my understanding that Seneca did not let wealth make a slave of him. It appears that neither exile, wealth, nor his ordered death swayed him or dictated how he was going to carry himself in life. This all seems to make total sense when I reread his quote from above.

Let us postpone nothing.
Let us balance life's books each day.
Let us prepare for glory.

What amazes me when I read about someone like Seneca is his ability to flip the script in any circumstance. He was sent into exile, yet he wrote a letter to his mother to console her. This reminds me so much of when, in the Bible, Paul is sent to jail, and he winds up writing numerous letters to various tribes and groups of people encouraging them, even though he is the one sitting in a cell. So when we think about resiliency, we must be able to flip the script on our circumstances. What also amazes me about Seneca was that even when he had obtained wealth, power, and influence, he made sure not to let it have dominion in his heart. In his writing *De Vita Beata*—meaning "On the Happy Life"—

Seneca states, "For the wise man does not consider himself unworthy of any gifts from Fortune's hands: he does not love wealth but he would rather have it; he does not admit into his heart but into his home; and what wealth is his he does not reject but keeps, wishing it to supply greater scope for him to practice his virtue." This comes from a man who was a political adviser to arguably the most powerful man in the world. Sure, take full advantage of wealth and use it in the best way possible, but do not make it your crutch. Do not worship at the altar of wealth and materiality.

Seneca had a fascinating outlook on life and how to view success, loss, and everything in between. I say all this to drive home the point that our resiliency and strength is sourced deep in our foundation of beliefs and perspectives. Seneca, Marcus Aurelius, King David, the writer of Ecclesiastes, and many more people throughout history have shown and demonstrated this. Our foundation is of the utmost importance because the pendulum is always swinging in our lives. We experience the highest of highs and the lowest of lows. Life seems to be a series of peaks and valleys with unexpected bends and winding roads. But without a deep foundational structure in the form of how we view things, life will toss us aside with zero regard. I don't think a single person is immune to it, and I do not think a single person is born without having to confront the enormity of emotions, challenges, wins, losses, and suffering found across the planet. Even those who are born with a silver spoon in their mouth cannot buy their way out of struggle.

Seneca says, "Let us balance life's book each day." I love that, because how many of us seriously do that? For many, one day falls into another and into another and into another until we get a weekend or a scheduled day off to stop and think or reflect. We wander in this sort of malaise, never stopping to recognize the severely limited nature of our time on earth. It is not easy whatsoever to enter the frame of mind it takes to balance life's book every day. For me, it takes reading, journaling, prayer, exercise, or sauna, to name a few. But it is in challenge that we find growth and renewal.

I have found so much strength and resilience in what the previous generations came to learn and write down. I hope you do too. My challenge to you would be to ask yourself: How much stronger would my foundation be if I lived with the end in mind every day? What kind of rituals can I create to reinforce this behavior?

TIME? WHAT'S THAT?

After reading Seneca's quote for the first time, I had a question for myself. Had I lived for thirty years, or had I been dying for thirty years? One of those sounds positive while the other is very dark and ominous, perhaps even somewhat confusing. It sounds kind of like the scripture from Ecclesiastes, which says, "Frustration is better than laughter, because a sad face is good for the heart." Is the glass half-full or half-empty? There is this word I always bring up, and that word is *perspective*. I have always been a firm believer that the sweets are not as sweet without bitterness. The harsh realities of life have the potential to make everything else so much more enjoyable. Our trials shape us, our barriers harden us, and our perseverance opens our minds to new possibilities. All else fades in the face of death. But am I living life or am I just existing on this material plane, slowly approaching my dying day? Which one are you? Have you been both? This, in my opinion, is the perspective I am always chasing after.

In my short thirty years, I have both been guilty of wasting my own time and energy and proud to say that, at times, I have lived and experienced life to the fullest. As we ask ourselves these questions and read these incredible passages of wisdom, we can see it all boils down to time and perspective. When I first researched content on the Roman ideal of memento mori, I had to rethink how I viewed my time. We all want to know that we truly lived. I know I do. But I had this troubling issue with time. I found myself treating it as if it were an unlimited thing. The goal to live each day with the end in mind had me thinking differently about my time here altogether. If we all walked around like that famous Nickelback music video of their hit song "Savin' Me" and were gifted the ability to see a digital display above our head of exactly how much time we had left on earth, things would be different. But we do not get the luxury of the digital clock time display in the music video. (By the way, why does everyone hate on Nickelback?) The timeline is finite, and my days are numbered. I am alive, and my death draws nearer with every breath. I find unlimited energy and perspective in this truth.

Each day, each week, we get to experience this life as a process of death and rebirth. Every day we are dying, inching closer to that final moment. However, this can be so empowering when we also know that this gives us the opportunity to shed the old ways of thinking, doing, and behaving so that we can experience the day's challenges and obstacles with an open mind and enduring heart. What can I learn from this day? How will this day's experience shape me? Each day we are alive makes the next that much more precious because we have drawn one closer to the inevitable. The number of remaining days has shrunk. Every hour, minute, and second we are alive, we should be that much more encouraged to step into our purpose and live in that awareness. So many people wander through their days, months, and decades in a sort of numbness, as if they were lost. They fold at the first sign of trouble. Their inner strength and resilience are nowhere to be found. I know because I have been there before. I have been in the deep trenches of endless wandering. But not anymore. It's not some magic pill or a material purchase that delivered me from that wandering. For me, God breathed life into my nostrils in the form of perspective grounded in glory. Grounded in memento mori.

In *The Discourses of Epictetus*, the Roman and Stoic Epictetus says, "I cannot escape from death, but at least I can escape the fear of it" (Long). This is huge, especially coming from Epictetus. Again, I am not a historian, just a major fan of history. From what I have gathered, Epictetus grew up a slave from a city called Hierapolis, a Greek city in Asia Minor located in what is now known as modern-day Turkey.[7] He was said to have walked with a bad limp, presumably due to his time in slavery. To be a slave in ancient times was nothing to take lightly. Epictetus would not have known much comfort or love. Yet he seemed to possess an immense resilience. He was apparently banished from Rome at some point and was said to have lived alone for many years as well. However, when he speaks of death, he says, "But at least I can escape the fear of it." How beautiful. He was known in *The Discourses of Epictetus* to have also said, "Happiness and freedom begin with a clear understanding of one principle: some things are within our control, and some things are not. We have no power over external things, and the good that ought to be the object of our earnest pursuit is to be found only within ourselves."

What about your life is outside of your control?

What's in your control?

What can you do about it?

Epictetus was a slave, yet I somehow know his name. Seneca was banished from Rome, yet I have read his letters. Paul from the Bible was placed under house arrest, thrown into prison, and beheaded, yet we know his name and his work. Their fame and recognition, although spectacular accomplishments, are not the only fascinating things about them. In my humble opinion, they wouldn't be known today if not for their resilience and their ability to recognize what was in their control and what was not in their control. There should be no fear where we have zero control. Where we may hold fear of death, we should replace that with gratitude. We should be grateful that, because our life is finite, we can be the most resilient people on the planet if we so choose. Because when we talk about resilience, I truly believe it is found and experienced in the daily grind of life, also known as the present moment. It is often created from the seemingly mundane twenty-four-hour day being presented to us. How can life be mundane if we are dying each day? Remember, every day that we are alive is one less from the total. For me, the answer is simple.

Life is actually not mundane.

Our viewpoint and perspective might be mundane.

The truth is different.

Your life is bursting at the seams with extraordinary complexity.

It is said that the atoms with which we are made were cooked up in dying stars. There are approximately thirty trillion cells all networking and communicating to be *you*. It is also said the odds of being born a human are fourteen billion to one. At a molecular level, human beings are producing electromagnetic fields and our bodies are performing fusion events, some say more efficiently than nuclear fission. We are made of stardust. It is we who make things mundane. We decide what type of perspective to have. Life itself is exploding all the time with energy and momentum. We are quite literally being hurled toward death, a death that ends the current experience we are having on earth. Between now and that moment, we get to evaluate what is in and out of our control and how we will proceed into the fray. How you choose to view your life is your prerogative. I just wanted to share with you how complex and amazing it is to be a living, breathing human.

I TOOK MY POWER IN MY HAND

By Emily Dickinson

I took my Power in my Hand—
And went against the World—
'Twas not so much as David—had—
But I—was twice as bold—

I aimed by Pebble—but Myself
Was all the one that fell—
Was it Goliath—was too large—
Or was myself—too small?

Discovering Our Strength in the Ether of Love, Death, and Possibility

WHAT DID YOU think when you read the chapter title? A little bit woo-woo, perhaps? I wanted to give some insight as we get further into this book. I do my best to choose words as carefully as possible. As you read the rest of this book, I would encourage you to think of the word *resilience* as an umbrella. Within this umbrella, we have two subsections that helped me better understand what it means to be a resilient person: strength and identity. I understand I could take this idea and drive it in a thousand different directions. There are a plethora of other words and ways to describe resilience; I am sure there will be plenty of critics who may point this out. Still, I believe that my message has come together uniquely through my voice to make its way to you. I was very specific with these words because I believe *they* came to *me*, not the other way around. As I was living my life in the full throes of creativity, the title came to me. Just as I described in the author's note up above (yes, please go read it if you haven't already), I had this moment of *ahh, yes* when the words popped into my head.

ONE OF THESE WORDS IS ETHER

We will explore ether, and also another form known as aether, in depth later on in the book. But in short, I believe ether is the space in between everything. There is physical space, spiritual space, and even cosmic space between two people, objects, or events. There is also the space in between you and your greatest victory or defeat. There is space in between you today and you on your final day. There is more to this space than just time. There is learning, growth, and transformation that happens between the you today and the you next month. Between the you five years ago and the current version of yourself today. We live on one continual timeline. We like things broken down nicely into seasons and chapters. Periods in a relationship, job, or school, perhaps. But my question is: What's in the space in between all of that? In short, I believe it is our strength and resilience. When we look back on any period or season of our life, we can be made aware of how much inner strength, patience, and energy it took to weather that storm. We can also look at what it took for us to get to that graduation day, land a new job, survive that toxic marriage, or complete the passion project. Right there—between us and the trial, tribulation, or victory—lies our strength and resiliency.

Here is an excerpt from an ancient letter to what was called the "twelve tribes scattered abroad," also known as the twentieth book of the New Testament, the book of James:

> Consider it pure joy, my brothers and sisters, whenever you face trials of many kinds, because you know that the testing of your faith produces perseverance. Let perseverance finish its work so that you may be mature and complete, not lacking anything.
>
> —James 1:2–4

If I am to pull out one takeaway from this scripture, it would be that I need to conduct a living autopsy of my own life. I need to dissect and review all of my seasons and days, and I believe it will reveal how much strength I truly have. It doesn't stop there either. This autopsy can reveal just how much possibility there is. It will reveal how much mystery and wonder is intertwined in our life. There is so much growth and learning happening, and at times we don't even realize it. "Let perseverance finish its work" is some of the coolest advice we can get.

THE AMERICAN CRISIS

by Thomas Paine
December 23, 1776

These are the times that try men's souls. The summer soldier and the sunshine patriot will, in this crisis, shrink from the service of their country; but he that stands by it now, deserves the love and thanks of man and woman. Tyranny, like hell, is not easily conquered; yet we have this consolation with us, that the harder the conflict, the more glorious the triumph. What we obtain too cheap, we esteem too lightly: it is dearness only that gives every thing its value. Heaven knows how to put a proper price upon its goods; and it would be strange indeed if so celestial an article as Freedom should not be highly rated.

THE CRISIS AND MYSTERY OF IDENTITY

I HAVE HEARD it countless times before. I'll be speaking to someone about an issue they are having, and inevitably the subject gets brought up—their identity. Who are they *supposed* to be? That is the big question they are trying to understand, and it is the same question I have tried to tackle for so much of my life. It would appear that our identity is a pretty big deal. I have known so many to struggle with finding an identity. When I worked in behavioral health, I dealt with so many young teens struggling with this. As a parent aide, I worked with adults experiencing the same thing too. I would sit down with them to go through our one hour of parenting materials, which would often turn into a miniature vent session where they would tell me all sorts of things. Oftentimes it would lead to this topic of not knowing who they are anymore or not knowing their purpose and value in life. I believe this identity issue is at the core of understanding one's purpose, and if you know your purpose, you have value for yourself. And if you have value, then you have resilience. Is it that simple? Maybe. Laying it all out there is simple, but the work it takes depends entirely on our ability to be open minded and diligent with how intentional we want to be.

ROLES WE PLAY

One area of my life where I fell into a trap early on was when I placed much of my identity in the varying roles I played. Roles are tricky. We all play different roles in life: mother, father, sister, brother, cousin, aunt, uncle, and friend. These are all amazing roles to fulfill throughout our time on earth. But if our identity is completely tied up in this one role, it can become consuming. Our role in our family or in our business is a necessary one to fill. You could even say fulfilling a role is a requirement in life. However, some may falsely cling to a role and believe it is their entire identity because it makes them seem important in the public eye. It gives so much perceived value, and where we find value, we tend to hold on. And why wouldn't we? Humans love to know they are valued and important. It drives us, fulfills us. When we play our role to the best degree possible, sometimes there are even rewards attached. If your role in life is a professional football player and you do it to the best standard possible, you can be awarded a massive contract. You can win the MVP of the entire league. You might get your number retired. You can win the Super Bowl and be the MVP of that game too. Our society has created a system of rewards and celebrations for those who play their role well enough. This celebration and the attention we get drive more perceived value, which drives us, and so on. It is the cycle of handing out golden carrots to those who are cherry-picked as the best fit. Now to be fair, I do not think there is anything inherently wrong with being a really good football player or business professional. We exist within a system that will reward you for that role and make the most out of it. Personally, one role that I fulfill in this life is as a writer, and I can tell you this: it brings immense value to my life. I am not going to embark on an anti-role speech and tell you that all the roles you play in life mean nothing and then provide some life hack or sell you an instruction manual for identity issues. Rather, this part of the journey has to do with flushing out identity, the roles we all play, how to use them, to stand firm in our foundation and to view them in a way that gives us access to our true and authentic self. Because I believe once we have this perspective of our identity, we are in a position to build the brick-and-mortar foundation of resilience in our hearts and spirits. I believe this is how the divine speaks to us about our true selves. It is not easy to figure out. It is not supposed to be either. We work at it over and over and over again. We get stuck and then we progress. We take two steps backward and possibly three or four forward until we grow a tad bit more each and every time.

JOBS

Many of us have jobs. Jobs are a necessity for our country and economy to function and thrive. Obviously, a big importance of jobs is financial reward. I am not ignorant of the fact that we live on an economic planet either. Money makes the world go around, and like I mentioned before, we need money to simply exist, let alone have fun and be creative. So when we discuss our identity, it is fairly difficult not to go down a rabbit hole around the topic of our jobs and careers.

You will hold many jobs in your lifetime. I know I have. When I searched Google for "What is the average number of jobs a person will have in their lifetime?" I found some interesting statistics. The first was this from Chris Kolmar: "The average person changes jobs twelve times in their lifetime, according to the latest available public survey data (2019)."[2] Another one was this: "The average employee stays with their employer for 4.1 years as of January 2020. Men hold 12.5 jobs in their lifetime, on average, while women have 12.1 jobs."[2] That's twelve different jobs we might hold and twelve different roles to fulfill in society. That is perhaps twelve different moments where someone thought that this might be *the job*. The place for me to figure out who I am and what I am supposed to do. But I have come to find out that is an unfair expectation to place on a job or career. You see, jobs are man made, and the world is not. Neither are we if you believe in any sort of divinity or higher power like I do. Jobs and careers can never deliver your entire identity; they are more like a piece of it if anything. They are a role we temporarily fill, and they always come with a shelf life. Like we saw in the earlier statistic, the odds are that you will leave your job to go do something else, and I believe you should. The older we get and the more life experience we gain, the more we change. Change is good. It can be painful and confusing, but it is coming whether we like it or not. We eventually get older, and at a certain point, we leave that career or series of jobs. These jobs that so momentarily define us are like tears in the rain. That is not to say they are meaningless. I just think we have given them unjust leverage over how we establish identity and, therefore, build resiliency in our hearts and souls.

A Google search brought me to this quote from a Yahoo article written by Rachel Cautero:

> Workers in the United States generally retire at around age sixty-four, though data shows that the average age varies by state. For example, the average age of retirement in Washington, DC, is around sixty-seven, while many states' average age is around sixty-five, such as Iowa, Kansas, Maryland, Vermont, and Texas. Other states boast even lower ages, like Alabama, Kentucky, and Michigan's sixty-three, or Alaska and West Virginia at age sixty-one.[4]

Let's do a simple thought experiment. Let's say you are a nurse, teacher, corporate professional, or blue-collar professional. This job/career you have means the world to you. You earn money for your family; it feeds them, it supports a certain lifestyle, and you are really good at it. Heck—let's say you are great at it. Everyone respects you at your place of work. Everyone in your circle of friends and family knows you as that job, that profession. This one role has become your identity. You work tirelessly, growing in this profession, and eventually it consumes most of your waking hours. Decades pass by; the clock continues to tick, and eventually you are at the retirement age mentioned previously. You retire. Now what? Let's say you have until eighty-five, ninety, ninety-five, and so on. You now have twenty or thirty years to fill in retirement. How will you spend your days now? We unfortunately break our life up as an adult into years working and then years retired. But you do not retire from being yourself. You retire from a job. You move on from that temporary role that you fulfilled. I bring this up because I have heard stories and spoken with people who handed their entire identity to a career, and when that career was over, so was their sense of belonging and purpose. What's worse are the folks who do not even make it to retirement before they lose this role that they have placed so much of their identity in. What happens when your entire being is dedicated to a profession, and there are recessions and layoffs? When a new boss comes in and pushes you out? There are people who are thirty or forty years old who lose their job and their identity along with it. They were a police officer, firefighter, schoolteacher, or welder, or they owned a small business and lost it. Their sense of purpose and belonging vanished along with it. Some people have no clue who they are without these careers.

I know that I had much of my identity placed in my job when I was the dean of students at a high school in Phoenix. I had worked so hard to earn that position and title. To lose it would be to lose something I held near and dear to my heart. My family and friends were so proud of me when I climbed to that level. The thought of losing it was terrifying. When people would ask me what I did for work, I was so proud to say what I did. The truth was, though, that I was and am so much more than that job or any job. If I had lost it, the sun would still set, the world would still turn, and I would still be Erik. I would still have all of my same passions, talents, and skills. I would still be blessed and highly favored, and that is true of you as well. The saddest part, however, is there are so many Americans struggling with their identity, purpose, resiliency, and mental/emotional health, and this leads me to another tragic statistic: the record number of suicides that happen each and every year in this country.

According to the American Foundation for Suicide Prevention, "Suicide is the twelfth leading cause of death in the US. In 2020, 45,979 Americans died by suicide. In 2020, there were an estimated 1.2 million suicide attempts."[14]

Now I do not bring up these statistics lightly, and I am not claiming definitively to know why it is happening at such a high rate. When we see a number that big, it becomes just that: a number. But they are not just numbers and statistics. Each and every single number was a human being. A living, breathing human being who walked the earth full of life at one point. It breaks my heart in many ways, and the reason I thought it was worth bringing into this chapter is because discovering our identity and understanding who we are is what I believe to be at the core of building resiliency in our lives. I have had countless conversations with people when this was identified as a major point of frustration for them. My heart breaks when people tell me that they do not know who they are and who they are supposed to be. But that is the question in life to answer. That is the game of life. Figuring it out.

As I struggled with finding and creating resiliency in my own life, I had to begin with my identity. It is not the easiest task, but seriously, the question we all get around to at some point is, Who am I? That is a great question to take on. The question has more to do with what we identify with, our purpose and place within it, and less to do with our accomplishments. Accomplishments are great, and they represent our efforts; however, I do not think they feed our daily identity and purpose. I know people with many wonderful accomplishments, and they have expressed to me in private that they don't know what their purpose is. They can't seem to find their identity in a sea of things they have produced. When I was growing up, I felt this way too. Even into young adulthood, and well...adulthood. I know exactly what it feels like to not be sure of my identity.

DENY YOURSELF

In the ancient, poetic, and often challenging scriptures of the New Testament, Jesus invites his disciples at one point to deny themselves and follow him. Matthew reads, "Then Jesus told His disciples, 'If anyone wants to come after Me, he must deny himself and take up his cross and follow Me. For whoever wants to save his life will lose it, but whoever loses his life for My sake will find it'" (Matthew 16:24–25).

I know not everyone is a Christian or holds a fundamental belief in God or religion, but think about this moment from a thirty-thousand-foot view. Before this scripture, Jesus is said to have just spoken to his disciples about his imminent death at the hands of the Jewish religious leaders. He describes to them that he is going to die. Peter pushed back in disbelief, and then Jesus delivers the response we read in Matthew for them to deny themselves. I think his disciples knew the ones in charge of carrying out such a death would most likely be the Romans, because they were the government in charge of the day. This was terrifying because the Romans knew how to deal death and torture very well. It was their denial of Jesus's imminent death that invoked such a response from him. Here we are again revisiting the certainty of death. Except this time, we are joining it with this idea to deny ourselves.

I can apply this verse to every single aspect of my identity. What does that mean to me? Could it possibly mean in order to deny ourselves, we must let go of the things we have previously perceived as who we are? Does it mean death to all of the things the world has told us have value? Death to the endless list of titles, certifications, industries, and trophies that we think give us security and to step forward into who we were intended to be in the eyes of God?

Who we are as a person is boundless, and our identity is more like a never-ending mystery of what we are capable of than any title modern society could give us. It is my understanding that when Jesus invited others to deny themselves and follow him, he was inviting them to deny their old way of life and living in order to completely give themselves to him and the ministry. This is what they were born to do. I should deny what the world has deemed important to me and live in a new and radical way. *Radical* means a way that is an outward expression of my talents, skills, and abilities. Live like the person I was born to be.

I realized that in order for me to deny myself and live in a radically new way that is in alignment with my values, passions, and natural talents, I needed to name all of the things that I love in my life. But first, I had to deny myself. For example, I had to let go of the notion that being the dean of students actually meant something. I had to rid myself of all of the outside thoughts and opinions. The reality is there aren't as many outside thoughts and opinions as I thought anyway, and they cared even less about my decisions than I thought. I needed to let all of my old ways of thinking—misperceptions, overthinking, worries—fall away. My resiliency sat at the pit of what I knew was true about myself in my heart. I am certain there are things you know to be true in your heart when it comes to your natural gifts. You might love to take photographs, make music, detail cars, build things, exercise, and so on. You might also have natural roles in life. You are a great listener or speaker, or you are the friend everyone knows they can count on. I knew what I was drawn to. It took me trying out so many different things, but the more I engaged, the more I learned about myself. And bit by bit, I knew more of what needed to be left behind and what I needed to explore more.

I know what some may be thinking. Deny myself? Death to old ways? On the page it sounds really great. Especially when hearing it preached in a sermon, written in a book, or spoken during a Ted Talk. But how do those words apply in real life? For me, I struggled with my identity and purpose for a number of years. It has been a source of great discontent throughout my life. It caused me to downplay my passions and interests. As a result, I would avoid standing boldly for what I felt called to do and who I was created to be because I didn't think I was the type of person who did those things. I would think that if I was too outward with my interests, I would come off as arrogant or an imposter. I cared way too much about what others thought of me and what I was doing. I didn't want to seem like a poser. I was afraid. Yet I thought I was being humble and staying in my lane. But I was giving in to what Steven Pressfield in his book *The War of Art* calls resistance. I was downplaying my own strength and identity. I was in bondage to the perceived categories of who I thought the world wanted me to be. Therefore, I was a shell of my true authentic self. This is when I decided to start identifying things in my life. I decided to start giving myself this identity that solidified who I was and what I did with my time daily. I stepped into alignment with my natural talents, skills, and abilities. All of which I believe were granted to me by a benevolent, all-encompassing, compassionate, and grace-filled being—God. The creator of all.

I am a husband.
I am a writer.
I am a Christian.
I am spiritual.
I am a servant.
I am a runner.

I am a brother.

I am a friend.

Just like it is listed here in this book, I literally wrote this out in my journal. I wrote it out so that I could see it and believe it. Now, my overall identity is plainly Erik Fladager. I know we just unpacked the section on roles, and yes, you could say all of these listed above are roles that I play. But everything I just listed makes up the whole of who I am, and they mean the world to me. These are all pieces of myself, and many of the roles that I listed were not roles I was once willing to be public about. As an example, for too long I was not public about my passion for writing. I was also not outwardly showcasing my faith. This was all due to an immature and false thought process I held that made me think I needed to always go along to get along. What I found out was this: when you have an identity, you have a responsibility and a duty to honor it.

Runners run.

Writers write.

Believers serve.

Therefore, every day I have a question to ask myself: If you are who you say you are, what are you going to do today? If I am a writer and I am a runner, for example, then my day should model that behavior. My day should consist of some rituals, habits, and disciplines that involve running and writing. If I am a follower of Christ and believe in the divine, then I need to spend some time in deep thought, prayer, and meditation—to be an extension of grace, empathy, love, and kindness. I need to feed my soul today and be a servant to others. I need to do my inner work with as much intention and energy as I do at my day job and other worldly obligations.

Where do you place your identity?

Is there a discipline or workload associated with it?

LYING TO MYSELF

Before this self-discovery, I was always able to convince myself that I had done or accomplished enough after a long day at work. I would go to my day job for the typical nine to ten hours. Eleven to twelve on a longer day. I am sure anyone can relate to the leaden feeling after a tiresome workday. For most people, when we are off from work, the thought of doing much else can and will feel a bit laborious. We might take it easy that day and possibly skip working out or working on other projects. We are tired, stressed, and want to seek a distraction. For me, it wasn't until I made up in my mind that I was a runner and writer that I developed a sense of duty to train and write consistently. Although running was and is still one of my truest loves in life, I hadn't yet named it as part of my identity. I thought because I hadn't done a hundred-mile ultramarathon, that meant I wasn't a real *runner*. This mentality is why it took me so long to write my first book. I was always telling myself things like, *I'd love to write a book, but I'm not really a writer, I wouldn't even know what to write about*, and *Where would I even begin?*

This was all false.

Truth is, I've always had a love and passion to write; I just never thought I had what it took to lean into it and give myself to it. But the more time I spent doing it, the more I fell in love with it and freed myself to be creative. I came to find out that my inner dialogue and my self-identity was one of my biggest obstacles in the way of me acquiring the type of resilience it takes to achieve greatness in this life. And by greatness, I mean acquiring the type of resilience that can pull us through anything life has to throw at us. A resilience likened to marble or granite. A foundation upon which to build our lives and to engage in the heaviness. I call it divine because I believe this resilience is emanating from the source, which is God.

So many of us are going through an identity crisis in our society. For some it is more of a total lack of identity. What I have learned in my experiences is that identity is completely interwoven and intimately tied to our level of discipline in life. The story we tell ourselves and the way we name things have so much power and meaning. When we label ourselves as someone who *is not* something, we tend to make it a reality. When we say things like, "I'm never on time," or "I'm not a morning person," they become automatically hardwired in our brain and spirit. We will assume the identity that we form in ourselves. Interestingly, if it is true of those negative things, then the opposite is also true. We can name *what* we are and *who* we are in a positive and meaningful way. According to writer Patrick Rothfuss, "It's like everyone tells a story about themselves inside their own head. Always. All the time. That story makes you what you are. We build ourselves out of that story."[13] That story is so essential and important to the creation of who we really are.

A great question for myself was, Am I disciplined enough to be that person in the story? Am I capable of denying all the false narratives? Can I become who I always was intended to be?

DISCIPLINE AND DAYDREAMING

I always knew that discipline was an area of my heart that needed work. I was familiar with the great Jocko Willink saying that "discipline equals freedom" and wanted more from myself. I think discipline is one of those things that for some reason we dread, yet it brings forth so much value to our lives. Having certain disciplines in our life can almost immediately improve any situation. Having trouble sleeping? Get on a routine schedule that works for your life and be disciplined enough to stick with it. In this stage of my life, I have a pretty solid routine. I get up at 4:50 a.m. Monday through Friday, and I go to bed between nine and ten at night. As I type this part of the book, it's 6:00 a.m. at Starbucks. On the weekends, I will get up between six and seven in the morning. Early to rise and early to bed. At times I stay up later and sleep in an hour. I'm not perfect. I don't have any kids; it is just my wife and me, so this is what works at the moment. I know life will bring its chaos in the future, and we will have to adjust. But it takes discipline. My first book, this one that you are currently reading, and any other project will only be possible if I can be disciplined enough to work on it every day or as close to every day as possible. It can be challenging, and it will provoke that part of us that sighs in frustration when we think about routines, structure, and relentlessness. But discipline is also *sacred*—a sacred and ancient practice. In *Meditations*, Marcus Aurelius writes, "At dawn, when you have trouble getting out of bed, tell yourself: 'I have to go to work—as a human being. What do I have to complain of, if I'm going to do what I was born for—the things I was brought into the world to do? Or is this what I was created for?'" [1] In the Bible we also have Hebrews 12:11 stating, "For the moment all discipline seems painful rather than pleasant, but later it yields the peaceful fruit of righteousness to those who have been trained by it." It is a sacred and ancient human tradition to be disciplined, and it is within the realm of discipline where we find larger pieces of ourselves and what we are capable of.

So much of our identity and, in turn, our resiliency in life is found at the depths of our soul where only the anchor of discipline can take us. It is here in this place and space where we have these *ahh* moments of understanding and breakthrough. When I ran my first marathon, I thought it would be impossible for me to run 26.2 miles without a single stop to stretch and refuel. To put one foot in front of the other for three hours and forty-five minutes with only the water in my CamelBak and some salt tablets. Some say that is stupid, but it was so important to me to make the effort and to accomplish that. I remember the feeling I had afterward as I lay on the grass at the finish line. My legs and back ached in a way I had never felt in my entire life. I smiled and was elated. I was in search of that feeling. That feeling is so difficult to find anywhere else. Discipline is what brought that feeling into my being, and it is discipline that will deliver it again and again.

As I made discipline a focal point in my life, it has never ceased to amaze me just how hard it is to stay disciplined. It can be so challenging to stay focused and committed to something. It was not until I wrote my first book that I realized I was lacking in this area. I thought I was a disciplined person because I woke up early, went to work Monday through Friday, went to the gym on a consistent basis, and did some household chores. Those are all disciplines that I was accustomed to and benefited me, but in order to do more and become more, I still had much to learn about discipline. There are things that we have to do, and there are things that we choose to do. We have to go to work and earn money. We have to do certain chores. Mostly any other pursuit in life is a chosen discipline. Writing a book or starting a blog, a YouTube channel, a business, and so on takes much more than a normal routine. It takes hour upon hour of hammering on the project until you see it through. This could be a process that takes months or even years. The results, however, rarely disappoint. It puts us in a constant state of preparedness. We are always beating on this thing that is an extension of ourselves, and it makes us ready for almost anything in life. We all have something to offer and become. We can develop and produce until the day we die, but it will depend on how serious we are about it.

Onto another question: have you ever downplayed your talents and gifts as a hobby? I have. I did it over and over and over. I was so used to it that it was just second nature to me. Whenever someone would acknowledge me or give any praise, I went into downplay mode and began to say what and who I wasn't.

If you are anything like me, you might at some point find yourself saying:

"Oh, I'm not like an artist or anything. I just like to play around and try my best."

"No, I'm not a poet. I like to write some stuff that comes to mind from time to time."

"I'm not a photographer. Taking pictures is sort of a hobby."

"Music is just my hobby."

"I'm no writer. I'm more of an aspiring writer."

The list goes on and on. I would often tell myself a story of all the things that I'm not instead of telling myself the story of who I am.

This leads me to ask yet another question.

Do you daydream?

In these moments when we daydream or actually dream about who we are or what we want to be, we are experiencing our soul's unchained passion. I have always been a daydreamer. I have dreamed about so many things in the past but never acted on them. In my first book, I tell my story of how I was inspired to go to South Africa to do volunteer work and have an epic adventure like so many people before me. It came forth because of a dream/vision I had. I literally was daydreaming of it, and I knew it was in my bones to go and make it happen. I remember reading a chapter in Mahatma Gandhi's autobiography about how life-changing South Africa was for him, and I couldn't help but dream about what it would be like to go myself. What would I experience? How would it change me? Impact me? What parts of me would come forward that I never knew were there? I used to daydream about being a writer. I would read books and listen to interviews and watch podcasts of people who wrote books or worked as journalists, and I would let my mind go and wander. I could see myself doing it too. Reading, researching, thinking, taking notes, writing things down, putting it together like a complex puzzle or a piece of art—I would dream of it all. These dreams give us an inside look at our most raw and authentic self. They open us up to our true identity, and we can uncover another piece of the mystery of who we are.

What does this have to do with resilience? I believe our identity, our authentic self, and the discipline required to pursue our daydreams is so important to me because these building blocks truly led me to my greatest foundations in my life. Using them allowed me to become resilient enough to endure everything the world repeatedly throws at me. Training for and running my first marathon took resilience. Working my way from an entry-level position to a position of leadership within an organization took resilience. Completing my first book took resilience. *Divine* resilience.

I felt embedded in God's love and strength. I was never alone. We are connected through my inner strength.

You see, I believe we are all created in the image of God. Although that may have numerous meanings depending on who you ask, I see it as the following: when we realize that we are created in the image of God, our identity is grounded in him. Our power is grounded in the divine. Our love is grounded in the divine. At the very core of our identity is strength and resiliency. We are tied and bound to resiliency at the center of our being. To doubt this is to doubt our creator. We should rather take joy in this truth. It means even if we cannot see our strength and resiliency in our current state, it does not mean it isn't there, ready to be unlocked. We are made in the image of strength, love, power, and resiliency. That is our identity. We should step into it and step out of what the world has elected for us. Though the world, or the unengaged, likes to measure identity based off of wins and losses, failures and successes, we are so much more than that. Not a single failure or success should define us. Trying to avoid failure or trying to obtain worldly success is a trap regardless. The truest expression of ourselves is seeking our infinite well of strength and love on a daily and ritualistic basis.

If nobody has told you…you are made in the image of a loving, kind, passionate, powerful, resourceful, and empowering being. A divinity that is within us all and gives us everything we need to reclaim our identity. We just have to cancel the noise of the world. The noise of the old ways of doing and being. We have to cancel out the buzz of social media, self-image, perceived successes, past failures, and unfair self-hatred. Reclaim what is already there.

DON'T QUIT

By Edgar A. Guest

When Things go wrong, as they sometimes will,
When the road you're trudging seems all uphill,
When the funds are low and debts are high,
And you want to Smile but have to sigh.
When care is pressing you down a bit,
Rest, if you must, but don't you quit.

Life is queer with its twists and turns,
As everyone of us sometimes learns,
And many a failure turns about,
When he might have won if he'd stuck it out,
Don't give up though the pace seems slow,
You might succeed with another blow.

Often the struggler has given up,
When he might captured the victor's cup.
And he learned too late, when the night slipped down,
How close he was to the golden crown,

Success is failure turned inside out,
The silver tint of clouds of doubt,
And you never can tell how close you are,
It may be near when it seems afar,
So stick to the fight when you're hardest hit,
It's when things seem worst that you mustn't quit.

Endurance

IT ALL STARTS with the Easy-five mentality. If you follow me on Instagram, you will probably see a daily post of a sweaty treadmill with the caption "Easy-five," "Easy-six," or something to that effect. Usually, five or six days a week, part of my workout routine is to run five or six miles followed by some type of weight training or pull-ups/push-ups. Then I top it off with a hot sauna. Most of the year, I run what I call an Easy-five until I get closer to a big challenge or race like a marathon, in which case the Easy-five becomes an Easy-six, -seven, -eight, or -nine—whatever the training requires. But the general rule of thumb is to do an Easy-five or -six at least five and usually six days per week. Some days, I look forward to it. Some days, I dread it. There are times when I think that there is no way I can muster the energy to get it done, and it would be much easier to just stay home and find something else to do. One great reason for doing my easy five-mile run is that it keeps me in shape. It can keep the love handles at bay. It doubles as my time to pray, meditate, and really feel inspiration. Some of my greatest ideas have come from these runs. Another reason, and arguably the most important reason why I do it, is because it keeps me tethered to who I am at my core. The Easy-five is actually not so easy. It beats on me daily. It tests my resolve weekly. It forces me to build endurance—

physical, mental, emotional endurance—and it opens me up to receive whatever it is I am supposed to feel that day. It's a mindset. It's a way for me to look at any situation in life, and in the face of adversity, flip it on its head and call it easy. Because if I can do an Easy-five, then I can do an easy five hundred words today and hammer on a book or project. I can do an easy forty-hour workweek and accomplish what I need to complete the day's mission. There is really nothing about life that is easy, and almost everything we do requires endurance. The Easy-five mentality I have built compels me to have the endurance required to navigate life. I post about it as often as I can—not to boast or gloat but to hold myself accountable to possibly inspire others. If others can wrap their mind around what the Easy-five mentality is, then maybe they too can find the thing that helps them build endurance.

I got the Easy-five idea from the movie *Without Limits*. It starred Billy Crudup playing the great American runner Steve Prefontaine—"Pre" for short. Throughout the film, he would always refer to his routine ten-mile runs as an "easy ten." Steve Prefontaine was my idol growing up. He was some wild, five-foot, nine-inch, hundred-and-fifty-pound kid from Coos Bay, Oregon, who ran like someone that had nothing to lose. He was not someone who was born on third base, he was not the right height for a traditional runner, and he didn't come from a family of gifted athletes. He was born with the gift of endurance and an uncanny ability to take a brutal amount of punishment and keep going. Prefontaine ran high school track and cross-country in the late 1960s, setting both state and national records in various distance races. In his senior year of high school, he was awarded a scholarship to the University of Oregon, where legendary coach and cofounder of Nike, Bill Bowerman, was coaching. After arriving in Oregon, Prefontaine went on to win multiple NCAA titles in cross-country and track-and-field events. In his attempt to qualify for the 1972 Olympics, Prefontaine set the American record for the five-thousand-meter race, running a 13:22.8, and he qualified for the Olympics in Munich at the age of twenty-one. (Five thousand meters is just over three miles, by the way.) In Munich, Prefontaine ran a gutsy race and took fourth place in the five thousand meter, arguably one of the best races of his life. I say this because his last mile was clocked at 4:04 minutes, and the winner ran a 13:26.4. It was four seconds slower than Prefontaine's American record. For Prefontaine to run a 4:04-minute mile in his last mile is nothing short of a miracle. If you are not a runner or familiar with the sport, then it may not mean much. But imagine after running two highly competitive miles already, being completely exhausted, and then doubling down on your efforts and running at what would feel like a full gate sprint to the common person for a mile straight. This is what Pre did to accomplish his last-mile split time in this race at the Olympics. And he did it against the best in the world at just twenty-one years of age. Most of those great athletes were older, in the prime of their careers, and more experienced. Even still, Prefontaine took this fourth-place finish to heart and was determined to come back in a massive way. After the Olympics, he went on to close out his Oregon career like a stud, becoming the first athlete to win a track title four years consecutively at the NCAAs. He was considered a favorite to win gold in the 1976 Olympics. Unfortunately, before this could happen, Prefontaine tragically died in 1975 before the Olympics in Montreal. After a track meet in Eugene, he went to a party and was in a car accident; he rolled his convertible, which crushed him. He was just twenty-four years old. His style of running and his level of endurance was on display all twenty-four years.

Why talk so much about Steve Prefontaine? This is not just because he is one of my idols, but because when I first had the idea to write this book, I was in the middle of a run. I knew I wanted to include scripture. I knew I needed to include the Stoics. I knew my own life had examples, but I thought it was so fitting that this idea came to me on a run and that one of my all-time idols is Steve Prefontaine, possibly one of the toughest people to have ever walked the earth. I truly believe that about him.

When I first heard about Pre's "easy ten" in high school, I could not get over it. The thought of ten miles being easy to run was so unfamiliar. It has taken years of life experience and maturity to understand it in a different way and to implement it into my life. I cannot get into Prefontaine's head and understand what exactly it meant to him, but to me, it solidifies what endurance is and provides a way to practice it every week.

What is your Easy-five? Could it be the same as mine—running five or six miles as frequently as I can, which has become a place for me to build endurance both physically and emotionally? Or is your version of an Easy-five something else? I would call on you to write down what your Easy-five is. It should be something that challenges you on several levels and something you can do four, five, or even six days a week. Not everyone is a runner. Maybe for you it's stretching, a walk, a bike ride, swimming, hiking, yoga, the steam room, or deep breathing. All of these things, if done with consistency, will build endurance. Call them easy even if they are not. Flip everything on its head for a change.

TEMPUS FUGIT

Earlier, we took a step into the world of memento mori. Now, I would like to explore another Latin phrase and how it may apply to our understanding of building and creating endurance. The term is *tempus fugit*, meaning "time flies." According to research from the website Effectiviology, "The term tempus fugit originates in book III of Virgil's 'Georgics,' where it was originally written as '*Sed fugit interea, fugit inreparabile tempus*,' which can be translated as, 'But time meanwhile is flying, flying beyond recall.'" [15] It is yet another reminder of time and our place in it. In a way, tempus fugit is an anecdote about procrastination and wasted time. The reason I believe it to be so important to bring up in this chapter is that so often I have made the mistake of giving my time away to unimportant and meaningless tasks. So much of my energy and willpower has been wasted on nonsense. All of my energy that could have been used in a more meaningful and intentional way was used to do meaningless things such as binge-watch Netflix, scroll aimlessly on my phone, or sit at a bar and watch professional sports. I could have used that same time and energy to benefit my life and add meaning and value instead of consuming endless so-called entertainment. I should have been focused on the things that brought me tremendous joy and the things that are difficult to do at times but make me a better person as a result. Remember, "time flies, so use it wisely."

As we question our endurance and evaluate ourselves, ask yourself, How much of your cup has been drained by nonsense? How much power do you hand away? How much time flies away in front of our face? Tempus fugit is a daily reminder that as time flies, we become aware of our priorities and the rituals we engage in that build our endurance and, therefore, lead to greater strength and resiliency. Now don't get me wrong: it is not all about how much you accomplish and at what age you accomplish it. Nor is it about looking around the room at your peers for comparison's sake, because that will drive you mad. It is a zero-sum game, and it is a lie. Everyone is living their own unique life with their own purposes and passions. Comparing accomplishments or anything of the sort has probably never made you feel great about yourself, and it is not a fair comparison. Looking at someone else and getting inspiration from them is another thing altogether.

I tend to look at someone like Steve Prefontaine and find immediate inspiration. I look at his life and what he did in the sport of running and can't help but think that he operated with tempus fugit in mind. Maybe not even intentionally, but the level of action and focused endurance he exuded was undeniable. He did everything with great verbosity and did not seem to care what anyone thought, not even his own coach at times. I do not want to be Steve Prefontaine. I want to be the best version of Erik Fladager. The version of myself that was put on the planet to do good things for others, serve, learn, write, run, love, heal, and any other word that describes what I am trying to do here. So I say make tempus fugit your cause and ambition.

ANCIENT ENDURANCE

It is my belief that everything being discussed in this book was as real to the ancient world as it is to us today when it comes to our time, endurance, resilience, love, creation, forgiveness, and ability to find the strength to go on. We know this is true because they wrote about it. They wrote books, letters, poems, scriptures, and other great sources of information to help guide us in our search for endurance and resilience. With that being said, I also believe everything we are after, in terms of resilience and inner strength, will be found in one ultimate source. That source for me is God and God's immeasurable love for us all. Naturally, I understand that the word *God* can mean a lot of different things to a lot of different people. Many view it in a positive religious light while many harbor a negative and sometimes even toxic viewpoint. Usually, it tends to be a result of an experience we've had growing up or an institution that did not honor sacred and ethical principles. But what I would ask of anyone reading this text is to have an open mind and heart upon reading the word *God* or any other word that refers to the Creator. If you have had negative experiences with people and institutions associated with the word, I can promise you I am not referring to a punitive, fire-breathing, judgment-filled conglomerate that knows your name yet calls you by your mistakes and mishaps. I am referring to a kind, empathetic, benevolent, and creative love which exceeds all comprehension of the mind, makes total sense of the heart, and touches our very soul. Even in the religious texts, we have a story where Moses asks God what his name is, and God just says, "I am who I am." I love that. So when I say I believe that God is the source, I am referring to a complex and often misunderstood being that embodies all of creation, connection, love, and grace.

The first scripture I want to cover—one I came across when I was reading the book *Waiting on God* by Wayne Stiles—is 1 Peter 2:20 (NASB 1995): "For what credit is there if, when you sin and are harshly treated, you endure it with patience? But if you do what is right and suffer for it you patiently endure it, this finds favor with God." What really stuck out to me was the idea that patience and endurance finds favor with God. I was recently at a professional-development day for work, and we had this enthusiastic keynote speaker at the end of the event. He goes by Dr. Bird, but his name is Stephen Birchak. He was giving a talk on happiness, and he told us that 50 percent of our happiness comes from a genetic baseline. He said the next largest chunk of happiness was 40 percent, and it comes from intentional behavior. The last 10 percent, which he shared with the crowd, comes from our circumstances. I had heard something similar to this before this keynote, but the words *intentional behavior* stuck out to me. There was a connection for me to the above scripture.

We choose to endure situations. Endurance is a very intentional behavior. We do not choose all of our circumstances, but we do choose our response. Then there are the circumstances we do choose, like deciding to do a triathlon or take up painting, build a house, write a book, and so forth. Regardless of whether the circumstance was intentional or not, our decision to suffer through something and be patient throughout is intentional behavior at its finest. To add to that, it accounts for 40 percent of our happiness, while the circumstance itself accounts for only 10 percent. I have wasted too much time thinking those numbers were reversed. I used to think the circumstances dictated my mental and emotional well-being and did not see the value in patience and endurance. I thought that, at best, it was a nice by-product of what we go through. Which leads to more questions to ask ourselves: Are we being intentional on a daily basis? What are our intentional behaviors? How much power is handed over to circumstances?

When I became much more forward focused on intentional endurance and patience, some things shifted for me. This is a concept written thousands of years ago in a completely different time with totally different life circumstances, yet it stood the test of time and made it in front of my eyes there in that scripture. This tells me that human beings have been wrestling with this notion of endurance and patience for some time and that our willingness to embrace it and build upon it can deliver true results. Marcus Aurelius says in *Meditations*:

> Do not disturb yourself by picturing your life as a whole; do not assemble in your mind the many and varied troubles which have come to you in the past and will come again in the future, but ask yourself with regard to every present difficulty: "What is there in this that is unbearable and beyond endurance?" You would be ashamed to confess it! And then remind yourself that it is not the future or what has passed that afflicts you, but always the present, and the power of this is much diminished if you take it in isolation and call your mind to task if it thinks that it cannot stand up to it when taken on its own.[1]

To put this in some greater perspective, Marcus Aurelius was, at one time, the most powerful man in the world, being emperor of Rome until his death in AD 180. So roughly two thousand years ago, this man was in charge of the greatest empire and was writing about being present, anxiety, endurance, and intentional behavior. I write about it because to suffer and be patient is to be human. It appears to be a human requirement here on earth, and that's the good news. It's not just you. You aren't alone. Not only do we all go through this and experience it, but also humans have been perplexed by it for literally thousands of years.

Now, we get to learn from it and grow through it. This is something to celebrate rather than lament. I witnessed too many others who chose to root themselves in their frustrations rather than intentionally ground themselves in endurance and patience. Try it. The next time something comes up out of nowhere, try telling yourself, "This is an opportunity," rather than falling down mentally and griping. This is not to say venting or talking about things is not a good release, but how much of our venting is truly therapeutic versus a toxic perpetuation of a cycle we have been stuck in our whole lives? Everything that comes our way is an opportunity to expand and grow into a greater version of ourselves. We do not even need to search out the opportunities for growth when we view it all as an opportunity. They will come to find you, starting today.

STILL HERE

By Langston Hughes

I been scarred and battered.
My hopes the wind done scattered.
Snow has friz me,
Sun has baked me,

Looks like between 'em they done
Tried to make me

Stop laughin', stop lovin', stop livin'—
But I don't care!
I'm still here!

What's Love Got to Do with It?

There are so many conversational directions to go in when we talk about the topic of resilience and strength. There are so many historical examples and so many ways to unpack it and learn about it. Everything laid out in this book has been how I have come to understand it, apply it, and felt it necessary to share with as many people as possible. However, it would never be complete without discussing this particular topic: the topic of love. More importantly, God's love. It would almost seem impossible for me to discuss strength, resilience, identity, death, and how it all applies without mentioning God's love in my life and in yours. Even if you do not believe in God, are agnostic, or are even a flat-out atheist, I am sure you either believe in love or have experienced it before. To experience love is exhilarating. I am sure you would agree, although we may just differ on its source. That is OK. It is not my job to deliver proof of God's love, only my experience of it and its undeniable relation to building strength and resilience in my life.

CORINTHIANS

2 Corinthians 4:8–9: "We are hard-pressed on every side, but not crushed; perplexed, but not in despair; persecuted, but not abandoned; struck down, but not destroyed."

Why start here? There are so many loving scriptures to choose from, especially on this topic, yet I felt the need to use this one. Maybe it is because of its relatability.

"We are hard-pressed on every side."

I have been hard pressed, but never crushed.

"Perplexed, but not in despair."

It is so poetic to read that line, as I have always prayed that God would stretch and *perplex* me. I don't know how it really came about. Perhaps I just thought it sounded really cool in the moment and didn't give it too much thought, but on the other hand, I believe words come to mind during prayer and meditation that have deep meaning. Meaning that maybe I did not know then but comes full circle now in order for me to make a greater connection. It has been in my perceived weakness where God has poured out his love for me. It has been in my most perplexing moments that I was able to receive love knowingly and unknowingly. So I pray to be stretched and perplexed over and over again, because I know the amount of growth my heart and soul go through each time.

My initial response to reading this scripture was all about strength, and we could take it in that direction. But as I reread it over and over again, I started to get something more. There is a major difference between being hard pressed and being crushed. There is also a major difference between being perplexed and being in despair. Crushed and despair sound like defeat, loss, and annihilation with little to no chance of ever recuperating. It is often how we describe the most defeated people in life.

"Persecuted, but not abandoned."

The more I read this, the more it was obvious to me that there is something driving this force within humans to be stretched but not broken.

"Struck down, but not destroyed."

I do not think it is because we are the fiercest or the most physically tough species on the planet. The truth is, in comparison to most animals, we are not that tough. I think our ability to bend but not break is rooted in something deeper and harder to understand:

Love.

There seems to be a collective human consciousness surrounding love. Throughout the five thousand years of recorded human history, love has been at the center. It is almost as if it is the gravity that holds the world together. Even in the very beginning of the Bible, we have the Genesis story, which describes our world being brought into existence through creation, not destruction. I don't know about you, but when I create things and make things, there is so much of my love being poured into it. We often say things like, "I put my heart and soul into this project."

To put our heart into something means to inject it with all sorts of love and meaningful intention. To create is to be deliberate. So when Genesis begins the whole story circled around creation, that tells me we were born out of creation, and if we were born out of creation, then we are born out of love. Love is what connects us to every other piece of the puzzle. To be absent of love is devastating; to be full of it is ecstatic, thrilling, sometimes overwhelming, but joyous and intoxicating as well. I am not sure one can experience peace without love. There is no joy without love. When I write, I know that every ounce of my energy sunk into the work is done with love and care for the work that is produced. I want you, the reader, to feel it and experience it as well. It is an open invitation to be impacted by something written from my heart to yours. It is to accept an open invitation to live in a way that is totally aware of the mangled and difficult nature of life but instead chooses to live in a flow state that connects us to our strength and resilience.

PAINFUL CONTROL AND LOVE

Throughout my life, I have constantly found myself holding on to some idea of control. Control over situations. Control over myself. Control over where things were headed. I tried to grip onto my life as hard as I could. This caused a lot of pain. It was exhausting. It did not come from a source of strength or love. It came from a darker and more selfish side of myself.

You see, I always had this idea that somehow, I could be in full control of how circumstances in my life turned out. I thought if I could just do x, y, and z, then I could control the outcomes to some degree. I could somehow control all of the narrative of my life and journey. There were many times when I was stubborn and devoid of patience and tried to force things to happen. I was and still am to some degree very stubborn. Some part of me still wants control. I want the perceived freedom that comes with it. My desire only serves to drain me. Not only does this thinking and behavior tire me, but I also have learned something else…I was never in control.

No matter how hard I dug in, I couldn't ever truly gain control over any situation. I would write it off as not being patient enough, smart enough, or skilled enough. *Maybe I just didn't have what it takes?* I would think. The truth was that I had the completely wrong attitude toward control, strength, and resilience, which meant I had the wrong attitude and thought processes toward things like happiness, joy, purpose, love, and everything else that distinguishes us as humans. The harder I tried to fix every situation in my life, the more it hurt when it did not go the way I wanted. I would hold tight and throw my entire weight into an idea or a relationship or a job, and it wouldn't work out. That stung. That hurt. It burned deep inside. It hurt because I had made up my mind that the thing I was trying to control would be my key to fulfillment and would allow me to feel whole. As if I was somehow incomplete and inadequate to begin with. It always left that annoying question of, Why? What? How?

Why did this not work out?
What am I missing here?
What do I do now?
How can I be better?
More exercise?
More books?
More emails and phone calls?
"Perplexed, but not in despair."
"Persecuted, but not abandoned."
"Struck down, but not destroyed."

Who has ever felt the massive weight of those questions before? Some of us, myself included, think that we did not have enough of this or that. Something was or is missing. This is not true. Not true at all. In fact, it is my humble opinion that our innermost power is actualized when we open our hearts and turn our attention toward perceived weaknesses. Moreover, I believe failure is the single most powerful tool in achieving the correct perspective on control.

Think of that circumstance, that person, or that stressor. Visualize how much energy you are burning on it. How much thought force is being placed on controlling it? Then imagine letting go. It is an act of surrender. This is no cowardly act either, mind you. To surrender our idea of control is to release it to a higher power. A loving and benevolent power that is operating on a plane you and I could only imagine in our grandest dreams. Release the grip. Open your hands and heart.

At times there were things I could simply not get over—people at work, the job itself, certain dramas in my life. I would pray and think that time was the ultimate healer. At times it can be. But I would find myself lamenting and venting about the same things repeatedly, realizing that I was not truly healed and I was still caught up in the impossible action of striving for control. Then, while running, it dawned on me one day: you have refused to let go. These have always been hard realizations for me because, as I mentioned before, I can be stubborn. It is like I know in the back of my head that I said I was over this problem; I want that to be true, but emotionally I am just not quite there yet. As it continues to eat away at me, I just keep saying, I'm OK, I'm over it, no problem here. But the truth could not be further from that. I learned that once I surrendered my situation to God, it was then free to go and do whatever it was meant to do. And so was I.

We cannot control what happens, the outcomes or the circumstances. All we can do is release them and know that no matter what happens, it was a blessing from God. It's not always that clear. An abusive situation or a toxic work environment where you get screwed over doesn't seem like a blessing. But what it did do was present you with an opportunity to learn, to grow, to overcome, and to move along the path. I learned I could save myself from wasting so much time and energy when I focused on surrender and not on control. I had so much more strength to keep going because I knew that, rather than try to control the outcomes, I could learn about their purpose, and in turn, could find more of my own. Rather than feel drained, I could discover energy. Rather than feel a sting, I could discover growth. Rather than become jaded and hopeless, I could unveil just how resilient I am and press on with even more of the journey.

An opening of our hands is an opening of our hearts, and an opening of our hearts is a beautiful step toward acceptance. We can accept our lack of control and acknowledge the chaotic yet stunning nature of life.

If–

By Rudyard Kipling

If you can keep your head when all about you
   Are losing theirs and blaming it on you,
If you can trust yourself when all men doubt you,
   But make allowance for their doubting too;
If you can wait and not be tired by waiting,
   Or being lied about, don't deal in lies,
Or being hated, don't give way to hating,
   And yet don't look too good, nor talk too wise:
If you can dream—and not make dreams your master;
   If you can think—and not make thoughts your aim;
If you can meet with Triumph and Disaster
   And treat those two impostors just the same;
If you can bear to hear the truth you've spoken
   Twisted by knaves to make a trap for fools,
Or watch the things you gave your life to, broken,
   And stoop and build 'em up with worn-out tools:

Let's Talk about Ether

Yes, we are in the final chapter of this thought experiment I call a book. With everything already said, I thought I would save this piece for the end. As you might have noticed, I think certain words hold great value. There is so much more value in them than is apparent in their given definition. The right word can inspire and invoke love and change in a person's heart, and that is truly why I have a burning passion for writing. You may have noticed in the title I used the word *ether*. When that word first popped into my head, I thought it sounded really cool. I don't know why it popped into my head, but that was the start of it. I thought it was a very cool and curious word. It then expanded beyond just being cool and mysterious. I knew it came to my mind for a reason. I thought it could be the bridge between us all.

According to *Britannica*: "Luminiferous aether—ether, also spelled aether, also called luminiferous ether, in physics, a theoretical universal substance believed during the 19th century to act as the medium for transmission of electromagnetic waves (e.g., light and X-rays), much as sound waves are transmitted by elastic media such as air."[3]

Yes, that's a mouthful and it sounds confusing. Full transparency, and if you can't already tell, I am not a physics major or anyone remotely qualified to talk in depth about physics and luminiferous aether. But I did feel compelled to investigate it. When we speak of ether, we are talking about ether among love, strength, our bandwidth of emotions, and our connection to the divine. More importantly, we are talking about how ether can be viewed as the literal, emotional, and spiritual space between us all. Physical space, emotional space, spiritual space. There is much to learn from the depth and vastness of this space or ether.

Life is a series of events, relationships, and decisions and a whole mixture of outcomes. It all begins with us and whatever is in front of us. So with everything that happens throughout life, you have yourself in one place and position, and then there is this thing in front of us. It could be another person, relationship, job, project, or obstacle. The endless series of things in front of us tests our strength and our resilience constantly. We are constantly bombarded with tasks to chase, chores to do, and goals to accomplish. There is always something directly in front of us. As we go about this cycle of bombardment, at some point we may begin to grow frustrated. We wonder how much more of it we can take or if it is worth our time and effort. It is my opinion that few of us take a deeper look into the space in between us and the thing stressing us out. Rarely do we take a deep dive into the ether that separates us and the traumatic event we just experienced. We experience something and then we move on. We keep pushing. We keep going. There is something seriously flawed with this type of strategy, however. I found out that I couldn't just keep pushing. Eventually, you realize you have nothing to draw from. The resiliency well is empty. I wasn't learning or examining life's precarious situations. I was steamrolling through them. Then I felt it—God's subtle yet affirming voice telling me to dig into the mess. I realized that sandwiched between myself and the stressful situation was an ocean of possibility and healing. There in the ether was something to learn from, and I could discover peace and, in turn, resilience.

A PERSONAL EXAMPLE

My first attempt at college did not go how I had originally planned. Naturally, I felt like I was a failure. Back then, I was an honor roll kid in high school and a varsity athlete in cross-country and track and field. I grew up extremely fortunate and blessed to have two parents who loved me dearly and did everything in their power to raise me with love, care, attention, and intention. They are a gift. But nobody's life is perfect. After high school, I had a plan to get a college degree and do the whole American dream thing. I went to Scottsdale Community College on a cross-country and track scholarship right out of high school. I was so excited. I was so fortunate. We already discussed how influenced I was by the great Steve Prefontaine; although I was not headed off to Oregon, this was my version of his legend. So when I arrived at Scottsdale Community College, it might as well have been Hayward Field to me. I was grinding out my first two years of prerequisites and getting to do the thing I loved most in the world. Run. Race. Compete. Be a college athlete. The dream. *My dream.* It was all so poetic on the surface, yet fragile underneath.

After two years of community college, though, I realized I was not going to be a division-one athlete and was no closer to knowing or understanding the age-old question of "What do I want to do with my life?" Scholastically, I was doing a general-studies degree, which I was hoping would help me understand what type of bachelor's degree I wanted to pursue, and in turn, dictate what type of career field I wanted to be in. Athletically, I had received letters of interest from smalltown NAIA colleges to run track, but I did not want to go to a small school in the Midwest. I had this thought that it was the middle of nowhere and far from family and friends. I had no interest. The deeper truth was, after two years in community college, I was burned out on the sport. I was training harder than I ever had before in my life, and I felt like I was worse at competing than when I was in high school. I had moments of personal greatness and flashes of improvement but nothing long lasting. I was growing increasingly frustrated with myself, the sport, and college altogether. I went into college having zero clue as to what I wanted to study, and by the end of two years, the painful truth was that I was no closer to knowing that answer. Unfortunately, I believe my lack of direction was a by-product of a school system that is not open minded, diverse, or challenging enough for young people. Kids typically go from grade to grade playing a memorization game and are awarded the next golden carrot until they are eighteen. Then they are asked what they want to do for the rest of their lives. Who actually knows the answer to that?

Yet I thought I was the type of person who was supposed to know what to be in life. I thought I had expectations to know. Others had expectations for me. I thought I wanted to go to a big university. I thought I wanted to get a degree in business and make people proud. That's what I saw others do. So I decided to go to the University of Arizona. My one year there was the loneliest I had ever felt, even though I was surrounded by friends. I couldn't have cared less about the classes I was in, the chance of going to business school one day, or my meaningless part-time job as a janitor. I thought I was alone. It felt as though everyone else knew exactly what they wanted while I was clueless. The sad thing is that it wasn't true. I was not alone; I only felt alone. But I felt depleted, and I just wanted to be distracted from the reality of life. Failure and doubt are like a poison. If you let them seep into your mind, they will slowly take control and wreak havoc on your life. That was happening to me, and it made me feel terrible.

But in the midst of all that loneliness was a was an encouraging internal voice. That voice I believed to be God's. I can't explain it or do it justice with my words, but I believe the spirit of God hovers around us all the time. When we are hurting, it's there. When we are winning, it's there. When we are happy, sad, or frustrated, it's there. So even when I felt low, God was there to nudge me. God was there to provide me with an invitation to cultivate and examine the space between myself and loneliness. The space between perceived failure and myself. I wasn't finished, and I wasn't a failure.

I have a hot take here: nobody can *be* a failure. We can fail *at* something. We can fall short of the goal we set out to reach, but we cannot become failure itself. This idea, "I'm a failure," is so categorically wrong in my opinion because it hands over all of your power in one sentence. It is toxic language to use. I wasn't a failure. I wasn't alone. Deep in the spiritual ether between my loneliness and the failure lay a truth. The truth is, I gave myself to something and learned I could fail at it. I ventured into an endeavor and was exposed. But the truth is that I felt pain; if I could feel pain, then I had an equal or greater capacity to feel love. To feel strength. To be resilient. It reminded me of this line in James 1:2–4, "Consider it pure joy, my brothers and sisters, whenever you face trials of many kinds, because you know that the testing of your faith produces perseverance. Let perseverance finish its work so that you may be mature and complete, not lacking anything."

It was there in that spiritual ether where I found truth, strength, love, and God. It wasn't a failure at all. It was a significant learning experience and one which would wildly prepare me for future events.

What is it that you have yet to examine?

What space can be examined between you and that breakup? You and your job? You and the business?

AN EXAMINATION

Max Heindel once wrote, "All things are in a state of vibration. Vibrations from objects in our surroundings are constantly impinging upon us and carry to our senses a cognition of the external world. The vibrations in the ether act upon our eyes so that we see, and vibrations in the air transmit sounds to the ear."[8]

If vibrations in the ether can affect our eyes to see and our ears to hear, then which vibrations are impinging upon our hearts? Are they those from our emotions, our minds? I like to think that, in my young adult days, there were vibrations all around me carrying important information in the ether. Between this depressing frustration and I were all sorts of valuable pieces of information. There were things that I could see, feel, hear, and touch. And there were things going on all around that were unseen. In between me and my struggles were vibrations in that surrounding space, and once I was willing to confront, listen, and examine them, I was able to see clearly what I needed to do and how to move forward.

I learned that it is vital to constantly examine our circumstances and well-being. Everything we go through, everything that we experience, should be examined. Many of us let life happen to us or at us. "This terrible thing happened to me," or "That other awful situation happened to me." It is true that many terrible things happen within our lives, and often we leave it at just that. We then try to move on, get over it, or forget about it. Life happens. Bad things happen. But so do good things. And all things should be looked at thoroughly. I think it is important to note that it didn't happen to you or at you; it simply happened. Often, it may have even happened *for you*, which I can understand may be a difficult concept to wrap our minds around. It feels counterintuitive. I believe it might be because we struggle to understand how anything bad that happens could ever be good for us. What good could possibly come from the horrific things that happen in the world and within our own lives? I do not think I am the most qualified to answer the question, but I will be brave enough to put my thoughts out there on the subject. Because if it can help just one person understand their pain and examine it in the vast ether of their hurt, then it is all worth it to me. The examination piece takes part in the ether or the space in between, which I keep mentioning. When something happens, examine it. This is not to confuse it with dwelling on it, mind you. To dwell or to sulk is much different than to examine, analyze, or study. Usually, in the immediate aftermath of something bad, it feels as if time has slowed or ground to a halt. The awkwardness, pain, frustration, disappointment, and confusing nature of what just took place is so right there in front of our faces. Almost as if it were taunting us.

The business failure.
The breakup.
The layoff.
The sudden death.
The long and painful death.
The lapse in judgment.
The dullness.

In that moment, time slows to a malaise. To top it off, we may even be comforted by familiar phrases. "Don't worry, time heals all wounds." Unless there is intentional behavior, does time heal all wounds? I am not confident that it does. This also leads me to think, if we are wounded, why do we need to immediately be healed and made whole? Maybe it is within this fractured and hurt feeling where we learn and grow. We are planted firmly in one spot, and there is this thing that happened in front of us. In the space between us and the thing could be a sea of pain and frustration. Within all of that pain comes vital information and questions, which lead us to great discovery and growth. This growth builds massive amounts of resiliency and perseverance. It is an intentional behavior.

There is the seen and the unseen. The Bible talks about this in Corinthians. One of my favorite scriptures is 2 Corinthians 4:18: "So we fix our eyes not on what is seen, but on what is unseen. For what is seen is temporary, but what is unseen is eternal."

Upon writing this section of the book, I reread this scripture during my morning devotional reading and journaling. It prompted the following journal response that I would like to share:

February 3, 2023

THE VISIBLE WORLD

I have never been so tired before now. I thought I had experienced *tired* before, but nothing comes close in comparison to the exhaustion I am currently facing. It stares me directly in the face. Pulling me down. Pulling me apart. In every direction. It is an exhaustion that makes you feel nauseous even though you are not even sick at all. It is an illusion. A powerful illusion. It almost hurts. It is *awful*. It makes me look back and appreciate my old definition of tired. It is all I can see. It is all I can feel. But what I see and feel is temporary. It is building something greater within my soul. It is building something eternal. I may be exhausted, but I am present. It may hurt, but it is finite. Its impermanence presents an opportunity to connect to something exceptional. It is all around us, unseen. No matter the exhaustion, there is life constantly surrounding me. It is there to give back energy, thrill, and life force. It is unseen yet eternal. For that, I am grateful. I am blessed and highly favored.

The world breaks everyone, and afterward, some are strong at the broken places.

—Ernest Hemingway

In Conclusion

THIS BOOK MARKS the second time in my life when I sat down and did deep evaluation, rigorous study, and self-examination. I attempted to create connections between ideas we all face in our own unique ways in order to turn it into a palatable book. It has been a major blessing to live a life of examination and connection. I am in no way, shape, or form the foremost expert on the subject matter, and in many ways, it almost emboldens me even more to be the one who puts pen to paper to work on these topics. My goal is to connect with people. My goal for the work is to connect with people. How does your story, struggle, hurt, and pain align with each chapter/section/part of this book? Where can you make connections and add to it as well? I see myself as taking part in a collection of ideas. You can take part in that same collection. Every time that you speak with a friend or a loved one and check in on them, ask them about their life, are there for them, or discuss these ideas, you are taking part in it. In every journal entry, blog, Facebook post, or Instagram post, you are taking part in it. The idea is for us all to talk more. Engage more. Discuss and challenge more often in a way that is both productive and meaningful. That is why I write these books. That is why I create the content that I do. When the idea for *Divine Resilience* came to mind, I knew it had to be shared. Same with *Our Soul's Path*. I think that strength and resilience is something desperately needed in our society. We all experience hardship and turmoil. Some say to be human is to suffer. But it is in the suffering where so much is found. It is in our suffering where we learn the most about ourselves and others. As a society, if we can collectively lean into hardship and suffering and use it to gain perspective and examine ourselves, we will be the most resilient people on the planet. We should be the most resilient people given the amount of recorded human history we have to learn from.

Lastly, I will leave you all with one final entry:

LESSONS IN HARDSHIP

> Come to me, all you who are weary and burdened, and I will give you rest. Take my yoke upon you and learn from me, for I am gentle and humble in heart, and you will find rest for your souls.
>
> —Matthew 11:28–29

Some lessons are only learned through hardship. Rest is not quite so rewarding if it is not earned in some ways. The things I think I want in life are not actually the things that build my foundation, character, or heart. A life of ease is not my goal. A life of learning is. I have prayed to grow both mentally and physically, and now I find myself in highly stressful and challenging situations. So I lean into you, Lord. I lean into your love and understanding. The mountain teaches more than the reward. Rest has never felt better than when it comes at the end of a long and laboring tunnel. It is here where I learn about myself. It is here where I learn about what I am capable of and where I must go next. I am but fruit on a vine, God. Use the various seasons to blossom my heart and ripen my soul in your divine image. Amen.

It is no wonder so many people of my generation and in the generations before and after struggle as I did and still do to this very day. But rather than seek the elimination of struggle or hardship, we should seek to build from it. Hardship is an infinite teacher. Suffering is a boundless tutor. To suffer is to be human. To doubt the process is natural. But do not rest on doubt, fear, worry, or anxiety. Look to what is greater, the person who will be born on the other side of hardship. The version of you that examines their own suffering and continues to calcify their mind in the realm of struggle will gain greater and greater amounts of resiliency in this world. I believe that God is teaching both of us in this way. Everything we pray for comes with a teachable moment and a trial. These trials are not easy to understand or comprehend. Yet these trials build in us a resiliency that is harder than diamonds. We should seek that hurdle. We should seek to build our perseverance and resilience in the ether of our love, our death, and our limitless potential with God.

Afterword

Embracing Life's Challenges: There
Is a Purpose in the Pain
By Martin Trevino

L IFE CAN BE challenging, filled with hurt, disappointment, loss, and pain. But guess what? You have what it takes to conquer it all. Your journey on earth wasn't meant to be a walk in the park. As Jesus said in the Bible:

> Here on earth you will have many trials and sorrows. But take heart, because I have overcome the world.
>
> —John 16:33

It is my belief that God created this world knowing it was going to be a difficult and challenging place. I also believe he must have put resilience in every living thing to foster the ability to overcome. Don't get me wrong, obstacles are exhausting. The feeling of constantly being beaten down by the troubles of life can take a toll on the soul of a person. There may have even been times when we thought we had it all figured out. Then, boom! Blindsided by a breakup or a falling out with a close friend. Maybe it was losing a job when you were just starting to make ends meet. No one is prepared for the sudden and unexpected loss of a loved one.

I can't tell you how many times I thought to myself, "When will I catch a break?" Have you ever asked this question, "Why is life so damn hard?" So many of these situations go beyond our control. What about the circumstances in your control, like preparing for a job interview that you desperately wanted but didn't land? How about the classes that kept you up at night, while working full time, giving every bit of yourself, only to fail the class? It's easy to lose hope. It's even easier to blame life for not being fair.

How do we find the willingness to draw close to God when we are angry with him? Circumstances like the ones noted above may even make way for the argument that God doesn't exist. It's my belief that these "points of contention," as Erik describes them, are in fact the tool used by God to draw us closer to him. It's in that closeness with the divine that healing, growth, and self-discovery is cultivated. In the 1940 book *The Problem of Pain*, written by C. S. Lewis (noted as his first major Christian work), he asks the eternal question, "If God is real, why do bad things happen to good people?" The answer to the question throughout his book is that God can use evil and pain to mold us and make us into who we each were made to be. This is God's love. And it is in his love, Lewis argues, that we can start to give a response to the problem of pain. But shifting our perspective to *What I am to learn from this?*

WHY IS LIFE SO HARD?

> Our Father refreshes us on the journey with some pleasant inns but will not encourage us to mistake them for home.
>
> —C. S. Lewis, *The Problem of Pain*

As human beings with feelings and emotions, none of us want to feel pain or discomfort. Whether it be the harshness of life beyond our control, the evil doings of others, or the disappointment of our own failures. The truth is those feelings and the thoughts that come with them can be crippling. For some of us, we do everything in our power to avoid those feelings. We'd rather chase happiness, ecstasy, and cheap thrills. Anything to keep us from feeling the pain of another disappointment. It took me twenty years to realize that not facing those negative emotions head-on was keeping me from being the person I was made to be. I believe this is what Erik is describing when he calls us to *push through the natural call of resistance.*

Life was difficult as a child. Drug and alcohol abuse and domestic violence was common in our home. These were circumstances well beyond my own control at my age. I did what most kids do in these situations: I tried to find acceptance and validation from peers. I was looking for a place to be seen and loved. The ways in which I chose to find an escape became coping mechanisms that dragged on to my adult years. Trying to numb my unresolved trauma led to arrest, addiction, and failed relationships. I had a belief that life was unfair. I became a victim of my circumstance and kept myself stuck, unwilling to confront the painful experiences of my past.

It wasn't until I looked for help that I was able to start to see my painful life experiences as something I can benefit from. Through faith, psychotherapy, and substance abuse treatment, I was able to start to see that life, although it was tough at times, It was myself that was responsible for keeping myself there, by being unwilling to push through and move beyond the disappointment of my circumstances.

ENTERING THE ETHER OF LOVE, DEATH AND POSSIBILITY

There became a point where I could no longer try to figure out life on my own. I looked for meaning and inner peace in many different facets of spirituality. Meditation, Buddhism, and Hinduism, to name a few. All very beautiful teachings and beliefs. However, as someone who was raised going to Catholic mass on Sunday with my grandma, I couldn't help but notice how much I was reminded of all that I was taught about God and how much of what I was reading sounded a lot like teachings Jesus spoke about in the Bible. I found myself seeking a Christian church, and that is when my life started change.

It took some time to start to build a relationship with God. I quickly realized that giving my life to God was not the same thing as meeting a magic genie who would take my problems away. Instead, it was meeting someone to give a meaning to my problems. I started to see a meaning to what felt like a difficult life. One of the hardest things to accept was that I was not in control. God was. As I do not believe that God creates the hard and painful things in our life, I do believe he calls us to walk through them in trust and courage.

I began to trust God's character. By discovering who God was, I was starting to discover myself. My strengths and weaknesses. I was learning to surrender. As the apostle Paul said in the Bible:

> And he said unto me, my grace is sufficient for thee: for my strength is made perfect in weakness.
>
> —2 Corinthians 12:9

Surrendering to God has been one of the hardest things to do. Yet, keeping myself from relinquishing control to my higher power, I kept myself in a space of resistance. In recovery we recite the short version of the serenity prayer, "God grant me the serenity to accept the things I cannot change, courage to change the things I can, and the wisdom to know the difference." However, there is a long version that finishes with, "Living one day at a time; enjoying one moment at a time; taking this world as it is and not as I would have it; trusting that You will make all things right if I surrender to Your will; so that I may be reasonably happy in this life and supremely happy with You forever in the next. Amen."

This is where I grew with God. In the belief that God was using all my pain, shortcomings, and disappointments for a purpose (Romans 8:28). This is where I found peace when facing challenges in my life (Philippians 4:6–9). It was learning to accept God's grace and to have grace for myself and others. I started to see trials as an opportunity to build endurance—as Erik notes with another one of my favorite verses in the Bible, "Consider it pure joy, my brothers, and sisters, whenever you face trials of many kinds, because you know that the testing of your faith produces perseverance. Let perseverance finish its work so that you may be mature and complete, not lacking anything" (James 1:2–4, NIV).

Gods endless love and grace + Digging deep through therapy and self-discovery = The greatest peace I have ever known. God is enough to heal us, but if we don't confront the pain we are feeling and understand the ways we are trying to keep ourselves from feeling, we will never discover the purpose that God has called us to fulfill.

REALIZING MY RESILIENCE

Moving forward was difficult. It was a long process. A continued process of healing. I didn't know that I was resilient in the moment; I just knew I wasn't giving up today. It wasn't until after I looked back, being asked to write this afterword, that I was able to realize my resiliency. Most importantly I now see what the purpose of the pain was all for—to grow closer to God and to help others overcome their pain. The American spiritual teacher / guru Ram Dass has a quote I love: "We are all just walking each other home." I first needed to find my way home—back to God. Through my own challenges and pain, I can use my experience to help others find trust and comfort in a higher power. I do this through love. Love for the human struggle, love for God, love for ourselves, and love for our fellow human beings. This is how we create a life of joy, peace, and meaning. That's when I discovered my purpose on this earth: to FEEL, EXPERIENCE, LOVE, and CREATE. I am to FEEL the loss, hurt, pain, and disappointments of life, just as much as I am to feel the joy and bliss. I am to use what I learn from those EXPERIENCES to show LOVE to others and to serve those who are hurting. This is how we CREATE a life of meaning.

THE DIVINE NATURE OF RESILIENCE.

What is it about us humans that we love an underdog story? The excitement of a buzzer beater in a basketball game. The rush of adrenaline we feel watching Rocky Balboa come back in the twelfth round after taking a vicious beating the entire boxing match. If you are anything like me, you must have played Wiffle ball in your backyard as a kid. No matter how long I played, every time I came to the plate to bat, it was the bottom of the ninth, with two outs against me, the bases loaded with a full count, and I was the winning run at the plate. I must have single-handedly won thousands of imaginary baseball games in my head. It's my belief that we humans love an underdog story because resiliency has been coded in our DNA. It's the nature that God intended. All things must have the ability to be resilient to thrive in this harsh place we call life on earth.

As I look to nature, I marvel over the strength that a tiny seedling must have to grow into a mighty oak tree. The resiliency needed to push through for hundreds of years. It was programmed by our creator and his intelligent design, to become what God intended it to become. However, our environment matters. If you took two of those same seeds and placed one in a favorable environment and the other in harsh conditions, they would have two very different outcomes. This is why the environment matters. I ask, What environment are you growing in? What type of nourishment are you feeding your mind and soul? What kind of people are you surrounding yourself with? Are they lifting you up, encouraging you, loving you when you struggle to find the sun? Or are they weighing you down and blocking the light you need to grow?

In my journey, as mentioned in earlier paragraphs, my environment wasn't always great. As a child I had no control over that, but as I grew older, staying in that mindset was now a choice I made. I would not be thriving and full of joy amid my current struggles if it wasn't for my environment. With 1,000 percent honesty, I write these last words as the sun comes through my window, two hours before surrendering to a forty-five-day jail sentence for trying to numb and escape my pain in a way that resulted in a DUI. My actions have consequences. But I rest in the comfort knowing God is fully in control. He goes before in all my troubles and meets me there with peace and strength. It's only by what I choose to feed myself (the word of God), the environment I kept myself in (loving, supportive friends and family who encourage me), the belief that God is calling me to a greater purpose in my trials, that in this moment I am as steady as an old oak tree!

I want to thank Erik for not only allowing me the opportunity to contribute to his second book, but for being an amazing loving friend, brother in Christ, and someone I admire and strive to be like. Your friendship and this opportunity mean so much to me. Especially at this moment in my life. You truly helped me on my journey. I will forever be grateful for you. Thank you to my brothers in Christ from CCV men's group (too many to mention). To Freddy Sandoval of Awaken Church in San Diego, California. To Christian G. for introducing me to Erik. Thank you to God for always loving me and guiding me. Thank you to my Lord and Savior Jesus Christ for his sacrifice and endless grace. It's because of you, that I AM RESILIENT.

Acknowledgments

ONE OF THE hardest things I have ever personally accomplished was to take a blank Word document and turn it into a legible book. I may be the author of this book, but it is not without help and assistance from many. So I first say thank you to my supportive family. You all support me so much and believe in me, and that has power that is indescribable. When others believe in you, it can take you to a whole other level. Mom and Dad, you have always loved and supported me, and your love is one of the single most powerful tools I have ever had. So thank you again from the bottom of my heart.

One person who has helped me overcome my own self-doubts and fear is my wife, Anela. You know all of my cautionary characteristics and push me despite them. You have truly no idea how much that means to me and what it does for me as a writer. Thank you, my love.

To my editors at Elite Authors, thank you for teaching me through the entire process. Every time I submit the draft for edits, I get this sense of excitement, fear, and nervousness as I wait for the manuscript to come back full of edits and thoughts to consider. I learn something new every single time. The process is the most important part of the work. You all have a hand in bringing this book to life and for that, I am eternally grateful.

I want to thank every writer and artist before me. I could write lists and lists of names of people whose work has inspired me. If it wasn't for others writing down their ideas and making beautiful connections, I often wonder where we would be as a society. Where would people be without writing, music, art, and poetry? In the time of artificial intelligence, some may think writing is a dead art. A past time. But I do not think so. I think there is something to the human spirit that cannot be replicated. The writers who have inspired me wrote with unparalleled *soul* and energy. I appreciate all of them for that. So again, thank you all from the bottom of my heart.

Lastly, I want to acknowledge and give praise to my Lord and Savior, Jesus Christ. It is through Christ that any of this is possible. Christ has touched my heart in the lowest of lows and given my life true purpose and value. Thank you, Lord. Amen.

NOTES

1. Marcus Aurelius, *Meditations* (Mumbai, Maharashtra: Sanage Publishing House, 2020).
2. Chris Kolmar, "Average Number of Jobs in a Lifetime [2022]: All Statistics—Zippia," accessed April 5, 2022, www.zippia.com/advice/average-number-jobs-in-lifetime.
3. "Ecclesiasticus," in *Encyclopædia Britannica*, online ed, accessed March 1, 2021, www.britannica.com/topic/Ecclesiasticus.
4. Rachel Cautero, "This Is When the Average American Retires," accessed Dec 18, 2022, www.yahoo.com/entertainment/average-retirement-age-u-140021169.html.
5. Epictetus, *The Discourses of Epictetus*, vol. 1, trans. George Long (New York: Scott-Thaw Co, 1903).
6. Emily Rodriguez et al., "Ether Theoretical Substance," in *Encyclopædia Britannica*, online ed., 2023, www.britannica.com/science/ether-theoretical-substance/additional-info#history.
7. Margaret Graver, "Epictetus," in *Stanford Encyclopedia of Philosophy*, accessed June 15, 2021, plato.stanford.edu/entries/epictetus/#LifWor.
8. Max Heindel. *The Rosicrucian Mysteries: An Elementary Exposition of Their Secret Teachings*, 2021.

9. Heinrich Ritter, *The History of Ancient Philosophy*, vol. 4, trans. Alexander James William Morrison (London: J. Haddon, 1846).
10. Gabriel García Márquez, *Love in the Time of Cholera* (Penguin, 2014).
11. Patrick Rothfuss, *The Wise Man's Fear*, illustrated ed. (New York, NY: Astra Publishing House, 2012).
12. Patrick Rothfuss, *The Slow Regard of Silent Things*, illustrated ed. (New York, NY: Astra Publishing House, 2014).
13. Patrick Rothfuss. *The Slow Regard of Silent Things*, illustrated ed. (New York, NY: Astra Publishing House, 2015).
14. "Suicide Statistics," American Foundation for Suicide Prevention, accessed November 15, 2019, afsp.org/suicide-statistics.
15. "Tempus Fugit: Time Flies, So Use It Wisely," Effectiviology, 2022, www.effectiviology.com/tempus-fugit.
16. *300*, directed by Zach Snyder (Warner Home Video, 2007), DVD.
17. Wayne Stiles, *Waiting on God: What to Do When God Does Nothing* (Ada, MI: Baker Books, 2015).

Made in United States
Orlando, FL
17 April 2024